FATHERS OF THE

GREATEST GENERATION

Nothing Between Heaven and Hell

Jim Little

Library of Congress Control Number:		2012908811
ISBN:	Hardcover	978-1-4771-1304-2
	Softcover	978-1-4771-1303-5
	Ebook	978-1-4771-1305-9

Cover Photo: On the firing line. Company L, Third Brigade, North Carolina troops
on the rifle range at Camp Glenn, 1910. (Courtesy: Patsy Henderson)

This book was printed in the United States of America.

To order additional copies of this book, contact:
Xlibris Corporation
1-888-795-4274
www.Xlibris.com
Orders@Xlibris.com
114955

Contents

for

Ben, Jason, and Patrick

Someday, when the full story of this battle can be told, the American people will thrill with pride in these magnificent troops upon whom a tremendous task fell. They were faced by the most formidable task that could be imposed upon them, the breaking of two double systems of the greatest defense line the Germans ever constructed. On the left of their attack, there was some uncertainty regarding the situation, and this increased the difficulty of their work; yet these troops, working under the enthusiasm of their high ideal, carried through their assaults, penetrated deeper than even had been intended, and delivered a blow which attracted the greatest part of the enemy's resistance. Beyond all question, they made it possible to break the defensive line in a position of the utmost importance to the Allied cause.[1]

Official Correspondent[2] for the Australian forces in France.

IT HAPPENED ON THE
HINDENBURG LINE

[1]   History of the 118th Infantry, American Expeditionary Forces, France, The State Co., Printers; 1919.

[2]   Although not attributed in the text referenced, Charles Bean (1878-1968), renowned historian of Australia, was the only official correspondent from that country in WWI.

PREFACE

It is a wonderful thing to get to know your grandfather. Mine may have bounced me on his knee, but I have no real recollection of him because he had died when I was two years old. However, I had heard several interesting facts about him: first, he was stationed on the Mexican border in the early 1900s; second, he fought in the First World War and was gassed therein; and third, he was a postman. Other than a few other minor tidbits, that's all I knew about Robert O. Little until the spring and summer of 2009, more than sixty-two years after his death.

I was parade chairman of the Memorial Day Freedom celebration in Thomasville and had noticed that there were fifty stones in a quarter circle at Veterans' Park honoring deceased servicemen and servicewomen. I thought it would be nice to place one there for my grandfather and asked past mayor, Hubert M. Leonard (Major General, Ret.), if it would be all right to do so. He readily agreed. That being the case, I set out to find out something more about him than I had known. I interviewed my cousins who had known him; read newspaper articles, books, and online materials; and visited many libraries and the National Archives and Records Administration II in College Park, Maryland, as well as the North Carolina Archives and History in Raleigh.

What I learned was, at first, unbelievable, not in the sense that the exploits of Company L from 1909 through 1919 did not happen but that the story had been buried in the past for so long. For example, in the book _WHEELS of FAITH and COURAGE_ (Matthews/Sink), written for the centennial, it was stated, "Who made up the company and what it did is not known." The ensuing brief paragraphs did give an overview of Company L, and that was all.

These men, boys really, who joined this National Guard unit were destined to help write one of the most heroic chapters of the Great War. None of them knew what to expect, of course; but the saga that was to unfold of which they were a part was, I felt, screaming to be told. They are not here to tell that story, so I felt compelled to tell it for them.

On Sunday, August 30, 2009, a family reunion of Littles was held at Unity United Methodist Church, where R. O. had been a member. None of his four sons were still living; but most of his grandchildren, great-grandchildren, and others were there. His oldest grandson, Herman Little, was not able to attend due to his health; but the rest of us dedicated that stone in R. O.'s memory, with Herman's daughter unveiling the memorial stone. It was a grand occasion.

Since that time, I have spent countless hours learning as much about Company L and Company A as I could. The following narrative is intended as a tribute to those men, and others, who served this country so well. It is not meant to raise their actions above any others, for there were hundreds of thousands from almost every state who served on the U.S.-Mexican border and millions who were under arms in the Great War. It is, rather, a story within a story of a perilous but exciting time in our history. This piece is also sort of an encouragement for other authors to find out about their particular hometown unit and write a similar narrative.

This project started out as a remembrance of my grandfather, but there was so much more that needed to be told, and the story just began to write itself. Therefore, in the following pages I have tried to give a history of the military company founded in Thomasville, North Carolina, and designated as Company L, "The Thomasville Blues." It was formed as a result of a national charter authorizing states to form these units, and almost every town of any size assembled a company of men from the area and became the North Carolina National Guard. It was quite natural that the important leaders of the fastest-growing town in North Carolina—Thomasville—would decide that they needed to have a National Guard unit also. Thomasville and Lexington would compete for the best young men in the rest of the county.

The unit served with distinction throughout its short life span of ten years or so from the first days in 1909 to the demobilization in 1919. It had been formed out of nothing, except the boys themselves, no equipment or uniforms; but it became one of the best National Guard units in the young century. Their distinguished record is buried in the pages of the history of the early part of the twentieth century, for the men are all gone now, and the memories of ones who knew them are quickly fading. Fortunately for us, a few accounts of their deeds remain, enough to give us a fairly good idea of what these men accomplished.

The story, though, is not just about the men from Davidson County, but about the whole of North Carolina, South Carolina, and Tennessee, and therefore about all Americans who fought in the Great War. From what these men did and how they served their country, the rest of us can draw great pride and admiration. In some ways it is the story of the Great War as seen through the eyes of these men, but theirs was a unique experience as will become clear in the following text.

To many historians, World War I was the most terrible of all wars. It certainly changed the world like no other war before or since. Having started almost a century ago, it seems to get lost in the history books; and to ordinary people, it is not as significant as its predecessors (the Revolutionary War and the War between the States) and the succeeding wars (WWII, Korea, and Vietnam), but as a result of the Great War, as it was called, nothing would ever be the same. Almost all major events of the twentieth century have roots in World War I. From the downfall of all of the monarchies of Europe and Russia, to the beginnings of unrest in Indochina, to the realignment and emergence of third world nations, all had their beginnings as a result of the conflict from 1914 to 1918.

Many feel that no good comes of any war, and they may be correct, but mankind is destined to fight them, whether comes glory and honor or misery and defeat. No nation engaged in war ever remains the same. So it is with world wars—there is no going back to the way it was. However, this war was the paradigm from the old world to the new. Not only did the world map change, but new weapons—machine guns, submarines, aeroplanes, and poison gas—debuted in this conflict, making this war inevitably more horrible as it progressed. The tactics practiced by the Allied and Axis powers were similar to our Civil War, but these new and terrible inventions assured destruction of human lives on a scale which could not have been imagined just fifty years before.

The young men of that time were caught up in the caldron of the Great War. Leaders of all nations involved bear responsibility for the carnage. The soldiers, marines, and sailors were just doing their duty. Letters sent home bear testament to the willingness of the doughboys to lay down their lives for their country. It is fortunate that the United States did not enter the war until 1917 with the bulk of the fighting occurring for them the following year. The British and French battling the Germans and Austrians did not learn soon enough the futility of sending men *en masse* against machine guns and other highly efficient killing apparatuses. Millions died in a vain attempt to push the enemy back a few yards only to have the ground gained retaken. It happened over and over again. By 1917, the combatants had learned this lesson. Then it was time for the Americans to tilt the conflict in favor of the Allies. It took less time, therefore, for the Americans.

That being said, the American entry into the war was no less perilous than that of the other allies. Many of the greatest battles after 1917 were fought and won by the doughboys and marines against a formidable enemy who still had the will and might to win. They fought with the tenacity that characterized us as Americans, the deeds performed on the battlefield both for honor and for naught. In these old-style wars, it really came down to the individual, one soldier struggling, sometimes in vain, to stay alive and to do his duty even if he could not save his own life. These men who depended on each other to survive and perform well under the most adverse of conditions should not be forgotten.

This short volume is not intended to give a history of World War I or the strained relationships with Mexico in the early part of the twentieth century. For those of us looking back from a century later, these men are the reality of what happened in our distant past. Look beyond the pictures of the soldiers in their funny uniforms and see people, men just like ourselves. Look at their eyes; look at their expressions; look at their faces. They are not just historical figures; but they are also real people with dreams, hopes, and aspirations, some never to be fulfilled, and not really any different from our generation.

So these men, every man or woman who has ever served this country, deserve to be thought of in just that way—ordinary people who were called to extraordinary deeds. My grandfather was among them and was my inspiration for writing this account. The more I learned about what these men did, the clearer it became that their story must be shared. After all was said and done, the battles fought, the tally of casualties, and the general horror of what war was in the past, we promised these men that we would never forget. This then is a remembrance of Company L, The Thomasville Blues, with a companion account of Company A, The Lexington Rifles.

I have found that the more I search, the more there is to find. I have made several new friends with relatives of men who fought in Company L through information included in this volume. There is still so much more information to be discovered, but at some point I had to try to put it all together in a narrative. I hope this book is a challenge to other author as well as descendents of veterans to find out about the doughboys and others who served our country so well.

History, for me, has never been primarily about events so much as it has been about the people in those events. Instead of masses of nameless men attacking an enemy, I have always seen the ordinary individuals within that mass. I wondered who they were, what they were thinking, and if they survived. Julius Lambeth, Harry Tesh, Sandra Yow, and others have kept the memory of their family members alive; and I hope I have done them justice. Thank you. That, also, is the purpose of this book.

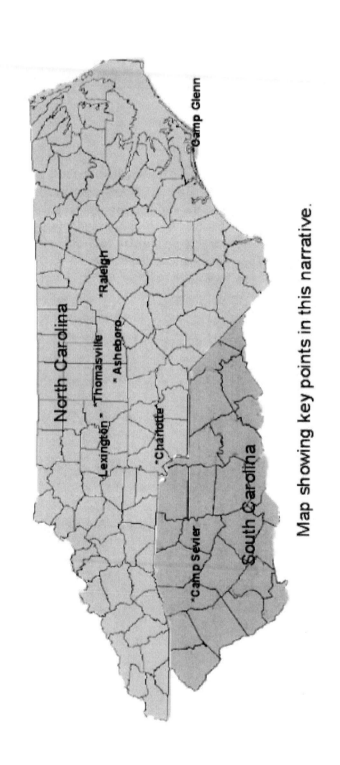

Map showing key points in this narrative.

ACKNOWLEDGMENTS

The bulk of the resource materials for this narrative came from Lexington's excellent newspaper *The Dispatch* from 1909 through 1919, accessed via microfilm at the Davidson County Library in Lexington. *The Dispatch* was diligent in saving all copies of their newspaper, but the same is not true of any of the Thomasville newspapers, which had been in publication almost as long. No known copies of the *Thomasville Times* or the *Thomasville News Times* exist prior to 1932. Neither the *High Point Enterprise*, which now owns the *Times*, nor the Thomasville Branch of the Davidson County Library, has any knowledge of copies prior to that time. Surely, if any copies are found, they will provide a rich harvest of local information not only for the gaps in this narrative but also for the entire history of the Chair City.

It is, therefore, truly fortunate that *The Dispatch* so carefully preserved their past issues. Had they not done so, much of the daily history of Lexington, Thomasville, and surrounding communities would have been lost; and the citizens of Davidson County would have been denied knowledge of some of their heritage.

Other sources were the North Carolina State Archives and History with the help of Lt. Col. (Ret.) Sion Harrington and the staff of the state archives; the National Archives and Records Administration (NARA II) in College Park, Maryland; the World War I Monument and Museum in Kansas City, Missouri; the Randolph County Library in Asheboro; Jay Harry Tesh, son of Clyde Tesh, Company L; Diane Murphy, grandniece of Hammet Harris; Yvonne Stewart, grandniece of Harrison Sullivan; and Patsy Henderson, who contributed many of the contemporary photographs taken by R. O. Little. Thanks also to the late C. Herman Little, who, before his death, spent many hours with me, helping me get acquainted with our grandfather.

The *Charlotte Observer* allowed unrestricted use of two photographs; the *High Point Enterprise* was used for some material; the *Asheville Citizen* newspaper was accessed through microfilm at the NC Department of Archives; and countless other sources both on DVD and written word were used.

Some online sources were used, but sparingly, since inaccuracy is unchecked on many of these sites.

Special thanks to Harry Lejda, PhD, for helping me with expanding the concept of the book. I have known and admired Jackie Sechrist, MEd, all my life, to think she would help edit my book—a true honor for me!

And of course, my wife, Pat, who encouraged me and was with me every step of the process from the idea to the finished product. She was with me everywhere, every hour of research at the libraries, every trip to Lexington, College Park, and Raleigh. Every time I needed her and swore that I could not finish this book, she was there. Without her encouragement, patience, and love, this story would not have been written.

INTRODUCTION

There were three brigades of the North Carolina National Guard. Thomasville formed its military company on March 26, 1909, as a part of the Third Brigade. High Point's military unit was formed in 1910, and they were assigned to the First Brigade. Asheboro's Company K, according to the Randolph County Heritage volume in their library, was formed on November 9, 1911. As of this writing, I have been unable to find the formation date of Company A, Lexington, although it was probably around the same time as that of Company L, based on the similar accounts of inspections and equipment arrivals.

The Militia Act of 1903 (32 <u>Stat.</u> 775), also known as the Dick Act, was promoted by United States secretary of war Elihu Root following the Spanish-American War of 1898, after the war demonstrated weaknesses in the militia and in the entire U.S. military. The primary sponsor of the bill was U.S. senator Charles W. F. Dick, a major general in the Ohio National Guard and the chair of the Committee on the Militia. On January 21, 1903, the act was passed by the Fifty-seventh U.S. Congress. The legislation gave birth to the "organized militias" (the National Guard), which were to be funded by Uncle Sam as long as they conformed to regular army standards within five years. The law stated that National Guard units were required to hold monthly drills and five days annual training. It also provided federal money for this training. Inspections by regular army personnel were also required.

The federal government had passed militia acts several times, but this was the first one which used tax dollars to pay for certain aspects of the law. The act also established a separate section of the war department to handle the National Guard's affairs. Major James Parker, U.S. Cavalry, was the first head of the bureau; and he had four clerks working for him. This forerunner of the National Guard Bureau was supervised by the adjutant general's office until 1908 when orders from the war department created the Division of Militia Affairs. Lieutenant Colonel Erasmus M. Weaver, Coast Artillery Corps, became the division's first chief; and the number of clerks rose to fifteen.

In 1910 the division was ordered to report directly to the army chief of staff. This was the arrangement until the passage of the 1916 National Defense Act at which time the Division of Militia Affairs was renamed the Militia Bureau of the War Department which then reported directly to the secretary of war.

~~~~

The American military is divided among the various branches which are divided still more, all the way down to the individual soldier. In the early part of the century as the National Guard was formed, each local guard unit belonged to a brigade—in the case of Companies L and A, they're part of the Third Brigade, North Carolina National Guard. It was in and of itself the organization and most of its units were located in the western half of the state, Durham's Company M being the notable exception. The Second Brigade generally was located in the eastern half of North Carolina and the First Brigade in the central. There were no hard and fast rules as to location, however.

At the beginning of the World War as the nation organized its military, more order was required. Therefore, Companies L and A became part of the United States Army and reorganized into that structure. The letter designations would not change, but all of the companies of the old Third Brigade became the 120th Regiment, and the old Second Brigade became the 119th Regiment; both of which formed the Sixtieth Brigade. The Sixtieth and Fifty-ninth Brigade, the latter made up of National Guard units from South Carolina, became part of the Thirtieth Division, which in turn was part of the Second Corps.

Originally being part of the Third Brigade, North Carolina National Guard, the two companies were very close kin, but when they were reorganized into the national scheme after 1917, their close association ended because the 120th Infantry was further divided into three battalions of four companies each (There was no Company J). Company A was part of the First Battalion and Company L part of the Third Battalion.

Simply put, the organization would be as follows:

Individual soldier > Platoon > Company > Regiment > Brigade > Division > Corps. Therefore when reference is made to the 120th Infantry, it would include all the companies A-M. References to Third Battalion would include Companies L-M but not A-D. Similarly, references to the Sixtieth Brigade would include 120th and 119th Regiments, and so on.

After 1917:

Companies A-D	➤	First Battalion	}
Companies E-H	➤	Second Battalion }120th Infantry}
Companies I-M	➤	Third Battalion	}

}Sixtieth Brigade

Companies A-D	➤	First Battalion	}
Companies E-H	➤	Second Battalion }119th Infantry}
Companies I-M	➤	Third Battalion	}

CHAPTER ONE

ORIGINS

Robert Orlando "Bob" Little was born in Cedar Falls, North Carolina, northeast of Asheboro, on October 10, 1888. He never knew his own father, Robert Edward, because he had died around the time his son was born. His paternal grandfather was also dead, but his great-grandfather and great-grandmother were still living nearby. His mother was called Mattie, Martha Jane Burrow, born in 1861, two years before Robert Edward. Both parents, having been born during The War Between the States, probably remembered only the Reconstruction era in North Carolina. Great strides in industry were made during their youth, and they lived at the time of the growth of the textile industry in the south. The most common occupation, of course, was farming and both were from farming families, but they may have met while working at one of the many cotton mills in the area. We do not know which one, but Mattie would have been a floor worker while Robert E. would have been a supervisor or foreman.

At the time of their marriage, May 17, 1882, the United States was experiencing what was called the "industrial revolution," a period of unprecedented growth and innovation in American industry which was to change the world. North Carolina was like most of the rest of the nation in this regard and, like most other southern states, remained largely agrarian, while at the same time becoming an industrial strength.

Bob and his mother apparently moved from Cedar Falls, northeast of Asheboro to the southeast corner of Randolph County for a while. A letter from his grandmother seems to indicate this, and Mattie's family came from there. About five years after the death of Bob's father, Mattie married a preacher from New Jersey named Jackson Wright. There must have been a simple reason that Bob kept his birth name, such as he may have been old enough so that his parents did not want to create any confusion, maybe his great-grandparents had an influence, or maybe it was just never considered at all.

By many accounts, Thomasville was becoming an industrial force in the early 1900s. The roads were not paved, and there were no sidewalks, but industry was flourishing in the city. Thomasville had become one of the busiest towns in North Carolina, and factory jobs were plentiful. The move from an agrarian to an industrial society found a home in Thomasville. There was a shoe factory which had been here since before the War between the States, also lumber companies, cotton mills, and several furniture-related factories including Thomasville Chair Company, Standard Chair, and others. In the ten years from 1900 to 1910, the town grew from 751 people to 5,000, an astounding rate of growth for such an area. Thomasville was also renowned nationally for its hunting retreat built by Col. Frank H. Fleer, the inventor of Fleer Bubble Gum, Chiclets, and a gum curiously named "Bobs." His company was first to include baseball cards in bubble gum packs in 1926. He had built a summer home south of town eventually called Fleer Mansion which still stands today. Fleer, himself, spent summers there.

The railroad, which ran through the center of town, brought passengers from all over the United States for the express purpose of hunting quail at the Thomasville Shooting Club. Membership was strictly limited to "upstanding" men of high quality. Most of the out-of-town guests stayed at the Mock Hotel, which was directly across the street from the station. Visitors would come for weeks or an entire season to Thomasville. Admiral Robert Peary, widely acclaimed discoverer of the North Pole, was probably the most famous guest, although one of the Firestones was a regular. Others included industrialists, evangelists, tycoons, even some royalty, and politicians.

Horses were the most common mode of transportation on the dusty (or muddy) streets, but a few "horseless carriages" kept the pedestrians and horsemen on their toes. There was no high school, but Thomasville Graded School stood on East Main Street. There were also several "graded" schools scattered around the area. The Baptist orphanage on the edge of town was run by John H. Mills.

Maps of the era show that there were very few if any businesses located along Main Street. A possible reason for this is the location of the "hog lot" adjacent to the tracks where the fountain and parking lot across from the big chair currently exist. Farmers brought their stock to pens located there for

Earliest known pictures of Robert O. Little. Top—At Camp Glenn with some of his National Guard friends. (Courtesy: Patsy Henderson) Bottom—R. O. at about age eighteen.

transportation to markets. A wise businessman would not want to locate across from such a place considering the odor and clamor created.

Salem Street was the downtown area. Many of the buildings constructed after the turn of the twentieth century still line the street. One section was called the "Burgin Block," for Mayor W. O. Burgin, and was adjacent to the current city hall. Another section was built by the Finches and still another by E. W. Cates, a city councilman and later mayor. Many of the buildings in this block had interconnected second floors, which could serve as meeting halls or sales floors. Evidence of stairways to the upper levels is still apparent today. Though most are in disrepair, some are still occupied.

The First National Bank was built in 1907, which was later enlarged and refurbished. (This building is now the city hall.) In the northward sections of Salem Street were fine residences of the well-to-do. South of the railroad on Randolph Street, there were a few buildings and some churches. This road would take a traveler south toward Cedar Lodge past the Glen Anna Academy for Women near where Ruby Tuesdays now stands.

In short, Thomasville was a prosperous little town. Although the Mock Hotel would eventually be torn down and the shooting club would lose its national appeal, the town itself would prosper, mainly due to furniture and textile mills, right through to the 1990s.

It was to this bustling little town which Robert Orlando Little came prior to 1909, probably for the employment at one of the many mills and factories. He was skinny by today's standards, but tall and handsome with blue eyes and sandy brown hair, and he made friends easily. The earliest account of his presence here was his enlistment in the newly formed National Guard unit which he joined at its inception. He had just turned twenty years old and was out to make his fortune just like most young men of his time.

From *The Dispatch*, Thomasville Department, March 31, 1909:

> Friday night [March 26] at the call of Mayor Burgin about seventy-five young men assembled in the Cates hall for the purpose of organizing a military company to fill the vacancy caused by the transfer of the Greensboro company from the Third Regiment to the Coast Artillery. About sixty enlisted, and Mayor Burgin was elected captain; Cashier Zed Griffith, first lieutenant, and Cashier A. H. Ragan, second lieutenant. The company is composed of the town's

best and most respected young men, and the officers are energetic young businessmen who will take a keen interest in the company and do all possible to make it the best company in the regiment. The company will go under the name of the Thomasville Blues.

Since this military company was formed by the mayor of Thomasville, it was held in the highest regard, and its success was assured by the addition of several bankers, very important men in any community.

What attracted young men to service with the North Carolina National Guard was probably the same thing that attracts young men and women today, a promise of adventure, camaraderie, belonging, etc. One reason given by some was the location of their summer camp, which was on the coast and would give them a vacation they might never have experienced otherwise. R. O. Little may have joined for any of the stated reasons, and he naturally was interested in becoming involved with a club of other young men. The extra income would also come in handy since he was to be married less than a year later.

The mayor, after all, was the instrument by which the military company was formed, so it is possible that his political stance might have been enhanced by becoming commander of a military unit. By all accounts, Burgin was a tight-lipped, serious, and humorless but a well-liked individual. Originally from Caldwell County, he came to Thomasville and started a career which carried him all the way to the United States Congress and was, at one time, an advisor to President Franklin Roosevelt. After the war and after leaving Thomasville, Burgin became a lawyer before heading to Congress. He would not be the first or last to enhance a resume this way.

A bank cashier in those days had much more authority and was generally a higher position than it is today. In fact, the cashier was considered a manager, and the men in this job answered directly to the bank owner or directors. So the commanding officers of the unit, Burgin (also mayor), Griffith, and Ragan were all men of some influence in the town. Burgin and Griffith were both from the First National Bank and Ragan from the National Bank of Thomasville. (It would seem that these banks were one in the same, but the reporter listed them differently.)

The naming of the unit, of course, was tradition at least as far back as the War between the States. During that war, the earliest militia units were also raised by men of wealth and position. Many funded the units personally and were elected to command the unit by default. The other "elected" officers were probably handpicked. Since the beginning of our new nation, military units were raised from within the several states and were given names that reflected some aspect of the town or some ideal.

Like sports teams today, the military units naturally had to have a name or a mascot. From where the name "Blues" is derived is lost to history as is the name "Rifles" for Lexington's Company A, but both were common enough from bygone days. This naming tradition would continue until 1917, when war was declared on Germany, and the National Guard was mobilized for service overseas, necessitating the use of men from other states.

Ironically, Company B of the Fourteenth North Carolina regiment mustered in during the early days of the Civil War was nicknamed the "Thomasville Rifles." A company in the same regiment from Lexington was called the "Lexington Wildcats." It is possible that Company A, Lexington, possibly being the earlier unit, chose the name "Rifles" leaving little else for Thomasville to choose.

The armory was the second floor of the post office known as E. W. Cates Hall. Cates's wife may have been the postmistress who took over those duties around the time the post office was located on Salem Street directly in front of the current city hall. Cates Hall was actually the second floor of one of those buildings on the east side of Salem Street. A postcard from that era shows those buildings, but individual identification is impossible. Similar structures today line the west side of Salem Street and give a good idea of what the others must have looked like. By 1913, the town map shows the armory upstairs at the corner of Salem and East Guilford, which today is a private residence.

As noted, prior to 1917, the Blues were part of the Third Brigade, North Carolina National Guard. The other units which made up the Third Brigade were Lexington, Raleigh, Henderson, Louisburg, Oxford, Franklinton, Reidsville, Warrenton, Burlington, Asheboro, Thomasville, and Durham. Detachments from Youngsville and Graham were also part of the Third Brigade.

Camp Glenn, named for Governor Robert B. Glenn, opened in 1907 and was situated in a very desirable location right on the water front at Bogue Sound, near Morehead City, North Carolina. There were only a few permanent buildings, and the troops generally camped in pyramid tents, eight men to each

William O. Burgin was mayor of Thomasville in 1906.
He later served as a state senator and U.S. congressman. (*The Dispatch*)

Camp Glenn as seen from Bogue Sound, ca. 1916.
(Courtesy: North Carolina Archives)

one. This was the attractive destination of all the North Carolina units each summer, one regiment at a time. (Despite the fact that the historical marker there today states the camp was opened in 1911, the earlier date is correct.)

~~~~

We have entirely too many bachelors in Thomasville, and we seriously hope a movement of some kind may be put on foot to reduce the number. Too many people of this class are a menace to civilization.—The Davidsonian, *June 24, 1910*

~~~~

The new company began training with a minimum of equipment and uniforms. It was not long, though, until Colonel J. M. Craig of the regular army conducted the first inspection of the Blues and the Rifles. He also reported in mid-April that uniforms and guns were on their way and would be issued soon. According to the reports, both of these units were made up of the best young men of the town who were trying to learn military tactics and principals in order to be the best company in the National Guard.

On July 7, 1909, it was reported that new uniforms had been received and issued. That was just a few days before the boys were scheduled to depart for summer camp at Camp Glenn. One week later, the rifles had arrived just in time for their first summer encampment. The trip to the coast was made by train. All of the boys had seen the train as it steamed through town, stopped at the local station, then moved on, but few had actually ridden on one.

Upon their arrival at Bogue Sound, the boys busily began setting up camp since training was to begin immediately. The days were long and hot, filled with the army way of training. Camp life need not be described for those who have served and know very well the daily routine, and it is lost on those who have not. It would suffice to say that the daylight hours were filled with marching, marksmanship, shooting, more marching, physical exercise, marching again, and formations. There is no report of the men using the machine guns at this camp which were to play so large a part in their future adventures. Most of the target practice was done using the new bolt action 1903 Springfield rifles which used .30-06 caliber ammunition. (The "06" refers to the first year that this ammunition was used.)

After the daily routine, the late hours were a different story. The troops were free to explore the ocean, go fishing, swim, or even go to the Atlantic Hotel in Morehead City for a night's entertainment. An electric train ran to other nearby towns. The hotel was the center of the tourist trade in those days and to the troops all summer as the different companies came and went. For most of these men, it was the first time they had ever been out of their home county. Most had never seen the ocean. For all of them, it offered a welcome change to the routine at home. Being a young man like R. O., it must have been a very exciting event. For the rest of his life, like many North Carolinians, a trip to the beach was an annual affair.

Eventually, though, the men had to return home to their jobs and families. For R. O. in 1909, he returned to his sweetheart and was married on December 22 to Maude Jenny Turner. They took up residence at her father's house which was near the present-day intersection of Liberty Drive and Trinity Street. Later newspaper accounts reported this as the "northern section" of the city, although it was more east than north. Nothing remains of the family home.

Having been founded near the same time, Thomasville's Company L and Lexington's Company A were naturally pretty close kin. There were cousins represented in each of the units. A newspaper article from *The Dispatch* indicates that it was suggested that the two sometimes met together about halfway between the two towns. Joint meetings were duly held and sometimes followed up by a big possum hunt, much to the delight of all the boys.

Thomasville's "Everybody's Day" was begun in 1908, also by Mayor W. O. Burgin, just one year before the National Guard unit was formed. In September 1909 it was reported that preparations were well under way for "one of the liveliest days ever seen in Thomasville . . . There will be a grand parade with nearly a hundred beautiful floats, also four military companies in dress parade. . . ," October 2 was set as the program date.

The third annual (1910) Everybody's Day was planned to be the biggest and best ever. The day was heavily overcast at daybreak, but by eight o'clock, the sun had come out and the crowds poured in from all parts of the state. By nine o'clock, parade time, three military companies led the procession from Randolph Street across the tracks, up Salem Street, left on Guilford, then left twice more to the starting point. One would reason that Company L was in the lead, Lexington's Company A and High Point's Company M (First Brigade) following. There were brass bands along with floats representing businesses and organizations. One curious float was sponsored by something called the Moonshine Whiskey Company.

Then the contests began: riding, shoe and sack races, and mule races. Everything from grapes to pears, pickles and yams were judged in the afternoon. W. A. Graham, commissioner of agriculture, gave a talk after lunch which was attended by a large contingent of farmers.

At three o'clock, the center of attention shifted to the field behind the graded school (located on the site of the future Main Street School built in 1922) where a sham battle among the three attending military companies took place. This was attended by many National Guard officers from around the state and one representative from the United States Army. High Point took the honors for the best drilled company. A fireworks display at 8:00 p.m. signaled the end of the festivities for the general public.

In the evening a formal grand military ball was held in the Mock Hotel sponsored by the Stonewall Club, which was to be the largest social event of the year. Officers and their ladies were in attendance at the hall which was decorated in red, white, and blue bunting. The attendees came from as far away as Reidsville. Some prominent names of those in attendance were Mr. and Mrs. Crutchfield, Mr. and Mrs. B. F. W. Bryant, Dr. and Mrs. J. W. Peacock, Dr. and Mrs. J. H. Mock, Mrs. H. Rapp, Elmer Fife, Mrs. C. A. Boggs, Mrs. J. F. Hayden, and Perry Griffith. Representing Company L were Zed Griffith, A. H. Ragan, and C. H. Newby. Of course, W. O. Burgin, in his capacity as mayor and host, was also there. There is no report of any enlisted men attending, but it is likely some did go.

Notably absent from the day's events and the evening ball was the state adjutant general Joseph F. Armfield who was seriously ill. On October 13, 1910, he died at his home in Statesville. The officers of Company L sent a letter urging Governor Kitchen to appoint Col. J. N. Craig to the position, but R. L. Leinster was appointed to the post a few weeks later by the governor.

Also in 1910, High Point in Guilford County started making overtures to Thomasville to form a new county with the former as county seat. Recognizing the potential of Thomasville's growth, proposals were made to unite the two towns under one county government. Negotiations were held, overtures were made, and discussions even went as far as to suggest a name for the new county, one being Ransom, (but "to be in Ransom is to set a price on our heads!") and another being Piedmont. One article that is quoted from *The Davidsonian* opined,

All this talk about High Point and its outlying villages annexing Thomasville, Abbots Creek, and other parts of good old Davidson is tomfoolery. If there is any annexing to be done, we will do it ourselves. If High Point is anxious to secede from Guilford county, Davidson might be prevailed upon to admit her. High Point would make a first-class suburb for Thomasville.

The whole enterprise depended upon High Point's willingness to pay for the proposed new county buildings such as the courthouse and the fact that Thomasville was happy being part of Davidson. The advantages of the new county would be that it would be the richest in the state being the center of manufacturing at the time. In the end, nothing came of the proposal, and the whole idea died quietly.

Target practice with the new rifles was of paramount interest to the guard units. The men held the Springfields in high regard (see cover), and Colonel Fleer's hunting lodge was probably the site of some of the target ranges. There were plenty of other sites in the county where it would be safe enough to shoot also. The sand dunes at Camp Glenn and the waters of Bogue Sound absorbed many lead projectiles as well, where competitions were held each summer.

An article in the *Davidsonian* for July 8, 1910, listed the names of the men headed to camp that summer—Capt. W. O. Burgin, 1st Lt. Zed Griffith, 2nd Lt. C. H. Newby, 1st Sgt. J. S. Burton, Quartermaster Sgt. T. H. Hilton; Sergeants H. S. Williams, A. A. Willliams, W. S. Morton, B. C. Turner; Corporals R. O. Little, E. O. Harris, Bob Marlowe, H. M. Bryant, and J. M. White; Bugler Wallace Stone; Privates R. J. Westmoreland, E. A. Stroud, C. V. Ward, J. T. Fowler, W. Veach, A. C. Kennedy, C. J. Lambeth, M. E. Bryant, Ed Cecil, T. H. Thompson, J. C. Sink, Frank Leonard, P. W. Stroud, J. B. Greason, J. G. Royles, C. J. Hill, C. J. Teague, M. W. Stone, G. E. Briles, J. G. Gray, F. L. Yow, V. S. Briles, W. H. Nail [*sic probably Nall*], M. T. Ownes, J. H. Kelly, and A. E. Perry.

Shortly after an altercation between A. H. Ragan and J. L. Armfield, the former resigned Company L to pursue other business interests in 1910. Both men were bank cashiers, and fisticuffs broke out between the two men over business matters. Neither party was injured much. Ragan may have resigned from Company L, but he remained active in the community, serving on the city council and as a judge in recorder's court. His brother was mayor of High Point a few years later.

The most remarkable thing about the summer camp of 1911 was that on the day the company arrived at Camp Glenn, it began to rain. In fact, it rained every day of the encampment, but there was never a complaint from any of the men who went about their military duties despite the wet weather. The men stood in their foxholes and dugouts knee-deep in water but carried out the orders given to them. The regular army officers in charge of the camp were amazed at their tenacity and cheerfulness despite the weather.

Back home, there had been a summer-long drought. This dry spell had idled factories in Thomasville because the river was so low that the electric facility was not producing the needed power to run them.

One of the perks of the encampment of 1911 was a moonlight cruise for the entire company up and down the coastline. All fifty-three men were treated to the adventure by Captain and Mrs. Wade Phillips, Mrs. W. H. Thompson, Edith Greer of Lexington, Mrs. W. P. Fife and her daughter Elmer, Ms. Perry Griffith from Thomasville, and Mr. and Mrs. Frank Page of Greensboro. The group rented two sailboats, the *Elwin* and the *Maggie Wade* for the occasion and picked up the boys at the camp for three hours, sailing up along the coast past Beaufort, Fort Macon, and the lifesaving station. Then they disembarked and went to the Atlantic Hotel where they danced and listened to the music. Very late at night, or early in the wee hours, the group then went back on board the boats for the return trip to Camp Glenn.

There was a very good reason that the Fifes came along on the trip because Elmer, sometimes incorrectly shown as "Elma," was to become the wife of Captain Newby. Her family was apparently well-to-do and hailed from Connelly Springs, North Carolina, although Elmer was born in Thomasville. They were married in 1912.

Major Wade Phillips and Captain James Leonard were both from Lexington, the former in command of the Third Brigade at that time and the latter in charge of Company A. Leonard was apparently well known in the county, owing to the prominence of his father, P. D. The elder Leonard had served as sheriff of Davidson County and was apparently well-to-do. The son was elected captain of Company A when he was only eighteen years old. He had a personal valet named Peter and, at some point, started carrying a cane, for effect, not because he needed it. Despite his demeanor, he was extremely popular, intelligent, and handsome and may have been mentored by Major Phillips. There is very little correspondence from Leonard, but Phillips was a prolific writer, sending many reports to *The Dispatch* for publication.

On the last day of camp that year, the military problem presented was carried out. The daily rain gave way to hot sun about noon as the men were assigned the particularly difficult task of attacking through a swamp so thick that federal troops had given up on it fifty years earlier. Using whatever came to hand, including ponchos, the boys from Company L battered their way through the swamp and successfully assaulted the "enemy." The officers observing were very impressed. Camp was over the next day, and the boys returned home to dry out.

In early January, 1912, W. O. Burgin was selected as secretary of the Greensboro Chamber of Commerce with a salary of $150 per month. He left a similar post in Thomasville for the new position, at the same time giving up his post as commander of Company L.

In an article from May 1912 is the first account of Carlton H. Newby (other than the officers' ball in 1910), who became commander of Company L and would remain so until near the end of the First World War. Burgin's resignation had resulted in Newby, then a first lieutenant, being promoted to captain. H. S. Williams was elected first lieutenant to replace Newby, and E. O. Harris became second lieutenant. At this time there were about fifty members of Company L. Newby set about getting the unit into military shape. His energy and drive made this company into one of the best in the state.

Newby hailed from Farmer, North Carolina, but had been in Thomasville for some time and probably was a banker at the First National Bank. About five feet eight inches tall, almost twenty-nine years old, with dark hair, he usually sported a mustache, wore glasses and a pocket watch with the fob looped to his belt. His demeanor gave him the appearance and bearing of an aristocrat, but his actions were those of the common man, and he was well liked.

The routine of twenty-four drills per year and one week at Camp Glenn was interrupted only once, that in 1912, shortly after Newby assumed command, when it was decided to go to Anniston, Alabama, east of Birmingham, for summer training. The men who had never been out of the state had their horizons broadened once more as they traveled through South Carolina, Georgia, and Alabama for their annual encampment.

Before leaving though, the company participated in the Independence Day celebration in neighboring High Point. The morning festivities included a parade by Company M, First Brigade (High Point), and Companies K (Asheboro) and L (Thomasville), both from the Third Brigade. In the afternoon Company L won the prize for the best exhibition drill which was held in front of the Enterprise office on Main Street. The public was greatly impressed by all the soldier boys.

Two days later the various units boarded the train for their next encampment. The train south to Anniston took the boys through Atlanta, then across the Alabama border to the Camp Pettus. There is no record of such, but the train probably stopped in the capital of the south—Atlanta—affording the boys their first view of that great city. If there was any time at all to explore, the boys surely took advantage of it.

The camp was situated on rolling hills about a mile square. Once again, pyramid tents were used for housing along with a few permanent buildings. Maneuvers and sham battles were held in conjunction with National Guardsmen from other states including Alabama, South Carolina, and Tennessee. Townspeople came out to observe the soldier boys go through their drills.

An account of the stay at Camp Pettus was written up in *The Dispatch* July 10, 1912, by a reporter with Company A.

IN CAMP WITH COMPANY A.
Idle Tales That the Boys Brought Back From
Alabama—None of Them Vouched For.

The Third Infantry, North Carolina National Guard, which includes Company A, from Lexington, returned from a ten days' encampment at Anniston, Ala. Monday afternoon. The ardent Alabama sun has made the boys swarthy as Hindoos, but they are all back, with no bones broken and nobody in the hospital and more than happy to be in God's country again. Their experience in Camp Pettus was rich, rare, and racy if the tales which they tell are to be believed.

The work of instruction was under the direction of Colonel Van Ausdale, of the Seventeenth Regulars, who was in command of the camp, and although it was hard at times, it was never overwhelming. In the forenoon practice "hikes" of from three to five miles were taken, usually with a sham battle at the end; in the afternoons, barring some routine work around the camp, there was usually nothing to do, and the soldiers were free to go where they pleased. The city of Anniston, two miles from the camp, held but few attractions, and thousands of the men hardly went to town at all; in fact, after marching from six to ten miles in the morning and fighting a sham battle, the average man was content to lie up in his tent and rest.

Company A, being the first in the regiment, was camped up close to headquarters, next to the band; the soldiers despised the band because its members never went on the marches, nor in fact did any of the hard work, and the interchange of compliments between A and the band was never ceasing. After lying up in camp all day, the band was naturally wakeful at night, when all the rest of the regiment was sleeping the sleep of exhaustion; the camp was on the side of a steep mountain, and the musicians had a pleasant habit of coming out in front of A's tents in the wee' sma' hours with an empty barrel, which they could fill with tin cans and roll down the company street, rousing the entire neighborhood and giving A a highly scandalous reputation with the rest of the regiment.

The sanitary conditions were under the supervision of Major Winston of the medical corps, and the hygienic rules were rigid in the extreme and enforced to the letter. Naturally, where eight thousand men are living within the space of a square mile scrupulous cleanliness is essential. In the center of the company's camp a fire was kept burning day and night, and every smallest particle of waste and rubbish had to go into that incinerator; failure in this regard meant fifty-seven varieties of trouble for the company commander, as every man in camp can testify. The extreme precaution finally got on the nerves of the men. It is said that one of the noncommissioned officers of Company A heard a tremendous row around the kitchen tent one morning; the cooks were all out fussing and wrangling and arguing at a great rate, and the uproar finally became so prodigious that he went out to investigate and found that the chef and the quartermaster had almost come to blows over the question of whether the sanitary rules required the lighting of a new fire or permitted the using of the old one, which was still burning!

The North Carolinians left Anniston Sunday night; early Monday morning a member of Company A, who shall be nameless for obvious reasons, became slightly exhilarated and strayed away from his company car. The train was running through a wild, desolate country, and nobody knew exactly where it was when the wanderer came through the car belonging to Company L, from Thomasville; he was picking his steps with great care and walking with wondrous dignity when a Thomasvillian roused up in his berth and after a glance out of the window said, "Say, what state are we in?" The Lexingtonian steadied himself and eyed his questioner with cold disfavor; when the seeker after information had wilted under his glare, he spoke in measured accents. "Sir, I," with a heavy accent on the "I," "am personally in a state of intoxication!" Wherewith he passed on and the Thomasvillian composed himself to slumber.

Among the propositions that have been definitely proved by the encampment are the following: A, from Lexington, is the promptest company in the regiment, being invariably the first to line up in response to a bugle call; M, from Durham, is the toughest, for they went out on the "long hike" with every man in line and brought them all back, yelling at the top of their voices on both occasions; L, from Thomasville, is the happiest, for they shouted and sang all the way on the slightest provocation and sometimes on none at all; and the miles in Alabama are the longest on earth, for the natives measure them as the crow flies, whereas the roads run as the angleworm wiggles. As to the relative heat of the sun and the feeblemindedness of the commanding officers, opinions differ, though everybody admits that both were appalling.

On the whole, A company is glad it went to Alabama, though none of its members are "raring to go" back—at least not this week.

They were gone a total of ten days instead of the usual seven or eight at Camp Glenn, and Thomasville was happy to have them home again. They acquitted themselves well while at summer camp, but there was never again a summer camp held out of state. Perhaps the length of the trip put too much of a burden on the working men of the unit, or maybe the expense did not justify the length of the trip to summer camp.

Once again, the best marksmen from the unit were picked to compete in a tournament in Raleigh. Corporal F. C. Rush represented Company L as high scorer with a total of 127 points, but no one from Thomasville placed in the winners' group.

~~~~

Archibald Johnson attended the big Finch picnic at High Rock last Saturday and made a good after-dinner speech to the crowd in which he stated that the "Finches" have solved the problem of capital and labor by treating their laborers as their equals when it comes to matters of kindness and consideration.—The Dispatch, *June 20, 1913.*

~~~~

On April 30, 1914, Robert O. Little resigned from the service and the next day was commissioned as second lieutenant of Company L. The resignation was standard operating procedure. Presumably Lieutenant E. O. Harris had resigned or had moved away. No record can be found to support either presumption, but Harris does not appear on subsequent rolls, sketchy though they may be. The commission elevated Robert to a leadership position and came with certain responsibilities, such as having to purchase his own equipment and clothing. A notation in his officer's diary from about that time showed $9.09 for a uniform. A similar notation was for a rifle—$22.50. This was a lot of money considering that a good week's pay in those days was around $30.

Uniforms were made of wool because of the durability of the fabric. The enlisted men were issued two sets which included the shirt, jodhpur pants, a campaign hat with cord, belt, hobnail shoes, and canvas leggings. Officers could opt for leather leggings which covered the calf from just below the knee to the top of their hob-nail shoes. Boots were rare and only a few officers had them, usually those above company grade.

At Camp Glenn in July of 1914, the qualifiers for the top honors in marksmanship were as follows: two expert riflemen, F. G. Rush and J. M. White tied with 220 points each out of a possible 250. There were seven who were marksmen: G. C. Jones, P. A. Shoemaker, J. B. Greeson, C. J. Teague, S. W. Newton, R. J. Westmoreland, and A. E. Perry. First-class riflemen were M. E. Bryant and L. B. Strayhorne. Second-class riflemen were S. A. Myers, C. H. Newby, J. T. Fowler, J. A. Stratton, E. D. Dorsett. L. R. Jarrett, and T. O. Ragan.

Rush and White scored the highest of anyone at the encampment, and there were more qualified marksmen from Company L than any other company in the Third Regiment. The criteria used for selection to the team must have been a complicated formula since Rush and White tied for the honor, but the latter was selected as the representative. Apparently, Rush would be able to qualify anyway at a meet in Raleigh, to be held October 12-13, 1914. Later that year, Rush and White competed once again in Jacksonville, Florida. White won third place overall, and Rush came in fifth. National Guardsmen from all over the southeast competed in the annual tournament.

The local company was always involved in community functions. On June 28, 1915, they fielded a baseball team against Thomasville Chair Company. Strayhorn pitched for the Blues and Newton for the chair factory. It was a great game according to the reports as the soldier boys won the contest 6 to 2. Also that summer, there was a company picnic at High Rock, hosted by Mrs. T. J. Finch, her sons Austin and Brown Finch, and Mrs. C. F. Finch. High Rock was a favorite destination for townsfolk in the summer.

~~~~

Mr. C. M. Bodenheimer has recently been having an artesian well bored at his residence in North Thomasville. When it had been sunk to a depth of 102 feet, he decided that if about 50 pounds of dynamite was exploded in the bottom of the well that it would break a fissure in the granite rock and would supply an abundance of pure water; so last week the shot was fired but without avail, so now all he has to show for the money spent is a nice round hole in the ground just 102 feet long. It is understood that he will give up the artesian well and run a pipe from the city water pipes to his residence.—The Dispatch, *Thomasville Department, November 11, 1914.*

CHAPTER TWO

THE SITUATION WITH MEXICO

(The history of this struggle in Mexico is too detailed for inclusion in this narrative. There are many books and online sources for the reader in case further study is desired. The summary presented here is merely to set the stage for the events leading to deployment of troops on the Mexican border.)

Mexico during the early part of the twentieth century was in turmoil, as it had been for many decades beforehand. The current troubles stemmed, as most revolutionary times do, from unrest over an oppressive leader. In this case it was a complicated series of events which led to Francisco Madero's overthrow by Victoriano Huerta, Pancho Villa, and others.

In the spring of 1914, tensions with Mexico came to a boiling point. There was even talk of all-out war with our southern neighbor. Captain Newby was trying to recruit a few more men to fill vacancies in case the company was called to active service. The newspapers were filled with alleged Mexican atrocities during this time. Reverend J. D. Newton volunteered to go with the unit provided he could hold church services away from any shooting. Once again, the pot did not boil over, and things settled down before any shooting began.

But the troubles did not end. National and local headlines in the period are filled with the accounts of the clashes between Mexicans and Americans. The Mexican port of Tampico was the site of one serious incident. Several sailors from an American vessel were arrested by a Mexican officer as they entered the town. The commandant of the area immediately released the men and apologized, but the captain of the ship insisted that he raise the American flag and fire a twenty-one-gun salute, which the Mexicans refused to do. A standoff ensued which was never resolved. Several deadlines were imposed by the Americans which were never met by the Mexicans. But soon this incident was overshadowed by the events at Vera Cruz, beginning April 21, 1915.

Mexico was a major supplier of oil for the United States, and Veracruz was the port from which the oil was loaded on tankers. A series of blunders, first by the Mexican authorities followed quickly by the Americans, led to an invasion of the city by the U.S. Military and resulted in several deaths on both sides. It was reported by wireless that a German ship laden with arms was en route to Veracruz. The weapons were intended for Huerta himself, and transports were waiting for delivery of the guns and ammunition, which included machine guns. Since at this time Germany was a belligerent in the Great War, there was a fear that these weapons would be turned on Americans. Secretary of the navy, Josephus Daniels, a North Carolinian, ordered the navy to seize the customs house and other key sites in that city and blockade the German ship, preventing it from landing, which was done.

All was peaceful as the sailors (who at the time were called "bluejackets") and marines landed and spread out toward their objectives, but resistance soon came from the Veracruz Naval Academy, where the Americans suffered several casualties. The big guns from three American ships in the harbor quickly leveled the academy, killing fifteen and wounding a large number of cadets. Many of the Americans wept at the sight of the young men who had perished, and some formed an honor guard for the bodies.

But the civilians were not forgiving and opened fire on a detachment of sailors in the town square, killing eleven Americans and wounding many more. In all, nineteen Americans were killed in the fighting. President Wilson was in attendance at the funeral procession and ceremony held in New York a week later.

By April 24, the fighting had ended with the Americans in possession of Veracruz, where they would remain for seven months. The German ship was turned away but off-loaded its cargo at another port. Eventually, the United States apologized for the incident, admitting that since no state of war existed between the two countries, the embargo was illegal.

The situation was volatile to say the least and could have erupted into a much larger scale of hostilities. During the entire affair, there was talk of sending the National Guard to the border in preparation for invasion of Mexico. Somehow, diplomacy prevailed and the situation simmered down—for the time being. The weapons never did reach Huerta, however, who was deposed and made his way to Germany. The only other thing that really changed as far as the relations between the two countries was that they got worse, but at least the Veracruz affair had fizzled out, and the two sides backed off from all-out war.

Raids along the Mexican border became common by both sides, the Mexicans to plunder and the Americans to pursue.

Once Huerta was deposed, Venustiano Carranza claimed the "provisional presidency," and Pancho Villa became his enemy. Emiliano Zapata, another revolutionary, was dead by this time, so the country was "governed" by Carranza with Villa in opposition. Originally backed and supplied by the Wilson administration because he did not drink or smoke, Villa had that support withdrawn in spectacular fashion when Wilson allowed Carranza to transport Mexican troops in American trains across American territory to do battle with Villa. Villa's army was almost wiped out, and his anger at the United States was unbounded. At this time the Mexican leader was located in the northwestern part of Mexico, Chihuahua province, near the Texas/New Mexico border. He was anxious to gather arms and ammunition to outfit a new army and to punish the United States.

During the first few months of 1916, the situation along the border became extremely tense. Villa had been raiding south of the border for some months, and Americans who crossed into Mexico did so at their own peril. Several were killed, and little could be done to stop him; but on January 11, 1916, Villistas halted a train at Santa Ysabel, and seventeen businessmen from Texas were removed and shot, execution style. They were mining engineers, civilians, who had been invited to Chihuahua by Carranza to Mexico with the aim of reopening some mines. One man survived and lived to tell the tale. Some said that Villa left him alive on purpose. After the train arrived in El Paso and news of the massacre was reported, the people went wild with anger.

American troops began crossing into Mexico in an effort to protect the United States from raids from the south. There were several skirmishes fought and several Americans killed, but many more Mexicans. An angry Carranza charged his army to "shoot any American headed in any direction but north" further alarming the Americans.

On March 9, 1916, still enraged by the withdrawal of support from the United States, Villa's men raided Columbus, New Mexico, and the nearby American Thirteenth U.S. Cavalry at Camp Furlong. Eighteen Americans were killed, and about eighty Mexicans lost their lives in the fighting. Several were later hung after trial. Two more raids into Texas resulting in American deaths finally prompted the Wilson government to act. Brigadier General John J. Pershing was ordered to pursue and capture Villa even if it meant going deep into Mexico to find him.

In January, 1917, Major Wade Phillips and Captain James Leonard visited Columbus to get a first-hand account of what had actually happened the day of the raid. What they were told did not make the history books. Three times Colonel Slocumbe, the commander of Camp Furlong, had been warned that Villa was planning a raid but disdained any information coming from civilians. Villa wanted horses and stole about ninety as the soldiers slept. A lone guard opened fire and was killed by the Villistas. This started a running battle with second lieutenants in command since Slocumbe was nowhere to be found. Ten soldiers were killed. In their flight, Villa's men then started firing on the town of Columbus, killing eight men, women, and children. The second in command, a major, begged Slocumbe to allow him to pursue the raiders, but the colonel adamantly stated that he had no authority to cross into Mexico. Thus ended the best chance to capture or kill Villa, necessitating the punitive expedition by Pershing into Mexico. Colonel Slocumbe was not disciplined and became part of the expedition.—Letter to *The Dispatch* from Major Wade Phillips.

Pershing and Villa had met before—in 1914. During the time when the United States supported Villa, they had actually held a conference and had an amicable discussion. Formal pictures were taken with the two leaders side by side and with both American and Mexican honor guards as they exited a building in El Paso, Texas.

On March 15, 1916, with the tacit approval of Carranza, Pershing entered Mexico at the head of five thousand regular army troops, mostly cavalry, and six aeroplanes. Charged by Wilson not to go too far and not to fire on anyone other than Villa's men, the mission was doomed from the start. The Mexican populace happily gave poor directions and bad information to the Americans. Pershing's troops were not to harass Carranza's men, only Villa's. Since the Mexicans had few uniforms, mostly civilian clothing, Pershing had no idea who was the enemy and who was not. Consequently Villa's men and much of the civilian population hounded the Americans everywhere they went. In towns, the subjects of the expedition were able to mingle with the locals and with the Americans, acting as friendly as needed, even attending movies with Pershing's men, in order to steer them in the wrong direction.

In June, the Americans were told that Villa could be found at a small village named Carrizal. On June 21, acting on this information, the troops charged into what turned out to be Carranza's men while Villa watched from a safe distance. This incident, which became known as the "Carrizal Affair," caused such a furor that Wilson was forced to call up the National Guard since war

Pancho Villa, center, and John J. Pershing at their meeting at Ft. Bliss, El Paso, Texas, Aug. 27, 1914. General Alvaro Obregon is to Villa's right and Lieutenant George S. Patton is to Pershing's left. In 1915, after most of Pershing's family died in a hotel fire, Villa was one of many to send condolences to the general.

Above: Villa and Pershing exit the conference flanked by Mexican and American color guards. (Both Courtesy: NARA II)

with Mexico seemed inevitable. The newspapers at home printed every detail of Pershing's exploits, further stirring American patriotism.

In the battle, Carranza had captured twenty-three American soldiers. When the Wilson administration learned that he was still holding the men, the president issued an ultimatum, demanding their immediate release. A deadline was given which passed without any action. Another warning resulted in the release of the men on condition that Pershing and his men return to U.S. soil. This latter part was refused, and Pershing remained in Mexico, but the incident did demonstrate that Carranza, at least, did not want war with the United States.

The Germans were delighted with the way Wilson bungled every opportunity of dealing with the Mexicans. The stage was now set for the next act in Mexican/American relations, but first we need to examine the European situation at the time.

CHAPTER THREE

THE SITUATION REGARDING GERMANY

(For an excellent account of this period of American-Mexican-German relations, the reader is referred to two works by Barbara Tuchman, *The Zimmerman Telegram* and *The Guns of August*. In them she gives a detailed and highly readable account of the troubles created by all sides from the period of about 1910 through 1918. As in the previous chapter, the purpose of this chapter is not to be considered an all-inclusive history, but only to set the stage for deployment of Americans to Germany in WWI.)

In late June 1914 Archduke Franz Ferdinand was assassinated in Sarajevo, causing Austria to declare war on Serbia. For more than a month, the already strained relations among the rulers of Europe and Russia were at the breaking point. The German ruler, Kaiser Wilhelm II, was the eldest grandson of Queen Victoria of England. English king George V and Tsar Nicholas II of Russia were also grandsons of the late queen, therefore, three of the five great powers in the first part of the twentieth century were first cousins. Many of the other sovereigns of Europe also were of English blood. Victoria's progeny also sat on the thrones of Greece, Romania, Norway, Sweden, and Spain, in addition to those already mentioned. Of the important houses of Europe, only France seems to have had no bloodlines from the late queen.

The kinship ties of the royals during this time made relations among them very cordial, even close. Each wrote to the other, mostly in their common language of English, in the most endearing and flattering terms. Wilhelm, particularly, wrote hundreds of letters to his kin including Victoria, her son, Edward VII; his son, George V; Nicholas "Nicky" tsar of Russia, and to a lesser extent the other cousins. Many of the letters from the German Kaiser offered advice in one form or another to his royal kin.

Wilhelm—Victoria always referred to him as "William"—was her oldest but not her favored grandchild, however. At various times throughout his reign, he was either very proud of his English blood or ashamed of it, and those feelings were always shared in England. At a royal wedding for Victoria's granddaughter in London, Wilhelm was placed far back in the procession being out of favor at that time, but upon the death of his grandmother, he claimed to have held her in his right arm (Wilhelm's left arm was withered and useless) as she passed away in January 1901, and he was placed in an honored position in the funeral procession.

Willy, as Kaiser Wilhelm was called by his cousins, seemed to be an intimidator with a complex and not thought of as being particularly well suited to the throne even by his own advisors. Being located in the center of Europe, Germans quite naturally felt surrounded by their neighbors. Through a series of alliances among other nations, Wilhelm felt more and more isolated from the other European nations. The *Entente Cordiale* (1904) between France and Britain which dealt with the security of the colonies of the two countries and the *Triple Entente* (1907) between France, Russia, and Britain was considered a threat by the Germans. With limited access to the sea, Germany was isolated but continually maneuvered to become the most dominant nation, expressed principally by the buildup of their navy. Claiming the battleships, "dreadnaughts," as they were called at the time, were commercial vessels; the Kaiser repeatedly denied they were belligerent. Everybody knew the truth, however. Meanwhile, Germany allied herself with Austria-Hungary.

Throughout his reign, Willy had tried to outmaneuver his cousins but was generally unsuccessful. Still, in the pomp and ceremony of the day, he was a force to be reckoned with and was accepted, many times reluctantly, in all the houses of Europe except France. The German alliance with Austria-Hungary became the catalyst by which Willy would, once and for all, establish his country as the dominant force in the world. The French would have to be conquered first, then the Russians who, by treaty, would likely come to the aid of the French. Russia was in no condition to wage war at all, and the Kaiser hoped his cousin Nicky would remain on the sidelines. England was the key factor to Willy. Would they come to the aid of the French, even though there was nothing to be gained for the Brits?

The invasion of France was all planned as early as 1905, long before the opportunity presented itself. Count Alfred von Schlieffen was Germany's chief of staff from before the turn of the century to 1905. Wary of France at the front door and Russia at the back, he developed the Schlieffen Plan should war ever break out. This was not just a contingency plan, but an active one waiting only for the right moment to be put into motion. Greatly simplified, the plan called for invasion of France through neutral Belgium. Before the Russians could mobilize, France would have surrendered, enabling Germany to turn her might on the eastern threat to her rear.

The French knew about the Schlieffen Plan and that Germany had drawn up plans for invasion of their country, so they too had a plan should Germany attack her. Their plan called for a counterpunch directly to Berlin from the southeast. The key to the whole puzzle was neutral Belgium. Germany would have to pass through that country for her plan to work, and France had to let that happen in order to call on her allies for assistance. France could not violate Belgian neutrality before the Germans did so. In other words, France was powerless to act before the expected German sweep of Belgium, which would put Germany on the doorstep of France before the latter could react. King Albert in Brussels and his countrymen, for their part, did not believe Germany would invade their country as it had declared its neutrality. For many years, it seemed that war was already at hand, but hostilities had not broken out. Neither power had any plan for static trench warfare.

It is truly ironic that leaders of all the countries of Europe, related as they were, would go to war with each other. It was not the assassination at all that caused the war, but the bluster and pomp of the various monarchies. The chest thumping, accusations, and innuendo went on from June 28 to August 4, 1914, when the first shots were fired by Austria. Wilhelm professed to his cousins that he was doing everything he could to prevent an Austrian strike, while encouraging the latter to do just that. Germany would support her ally, Austria, if she should fire on Serbia. Eventually called "The Great War," "The War to End All Wars," and "World War I," the slaughter of millions began at the whim of the belligerent leaders. That is not to say that the German populace were opposed to war; they did want war and threw themselves into it with all the enthusiasm and pomp they could muster, but to the kaiser, the death of the archduke and his wife was only the means to finally instigate the war which everyone knew was coming.

In the United States, the archduke's demise was reported in all the newspapers, and the story unfolding abroad was followed with great interest. Interest, yes, but the American people were not bothered enough to get involved. After all, this was a European affair which did not concern the United States. Instead, President Woodrow Wilson was determined to keep the country out of war with the Europeans and the Mexicans, no matter what the cost. In his "progressive" mind-set, he was the "great arbitrator," the salvation of the modern world, and he was determined to negotiate the settlement of the ages. He imagined that he alone would negotiate peace among the Europeans; but Germany, France, Austria-Hungary, Russia, and the rest of the combatants did not see it that way.

At this time, America was still enjoying the industrial revolution. The modern era was in full swing, and life was good for its citizens. Automobiles, aeroplanes, modern equipment, household appliances, and many other innovations and inventions kept American factories humming. The United States had little time for a war in Europe. There was even some question as to whom we would ally ourselves should America be forced into war.

Arthur Zimmerman (October 5, 1864-June 6, 1940) German State Secretary for Foreign Affairs 1916-17. Popular on both sides of the Atlantic until publication of the telegrams to Mexico. Subsequently instrumental in similar activities furthering Germany's war effort in Ireland and Russia.

By the end of 1916, the Germans, Austro-Hungarians, and the other great powers were aware that the war was not going well for them. Both began to realize that the war must be won quickly, or it could not be won at all. The thinking of the German high command was to win the war by going all out, or at least to force a favorable treaty, by a series of offensives aimed at destroying the French, Belgian, and British forces before America could enter the war and tip the uneasy balance in favor of the Allies. Germany had sunk many American ships, some just off the eastern seaboard, from almost the beginning of hostilities. America had protested through diplomatic channels, and the Germans had claimed one thing, then another, with a promise never to do it again. This was the pattern for the Wilson administration.

In late 1916, Germany secretly decided to resume unrestricted submarine warfare on all shipping, hoping to starve Britain and France out of the war before the United States could react. The targeted shipping would include American vessels which Germany declared were supplying the Allies. This was the plan. Of course, in true Prussian thinking, the Americans were considered only flyweights anyway so that even if they were able to send large numbers of troops, the Germans could brush them away like so many flies. The target date for the resumption of sinking of all merchant ships, including American, was February 1, 1917, and was announced by the Germans in mid-January.

This was not the only strategy employed by the Germans. As early as 1914, it was reported that Germany was urging Japan, an Allied power who had fought the Germans for the British in China, to switch sides and form an alliance with the Mexicans. Of course, the Mexican government itself was a moving target at that time, so it was difficult for the Germans to determine just who was in charge. After his overthrow, Huerta had taken refuge in Germany. Villa temporarily held the upper hand and had the support of the Americans. He was in no mood to betray his friends north of the border and said so to a Japanese diplomat.

Germany's overtures to Japan to change sides or encourage an alliance with Mexico seemed to have been realized when there were reports that Japanese warships had landed on the coast of lower California (Baja) and that the Japanese had been warmly received by the Mexicans. This was in April 1915. Whether this actually happened or not was secondary to its effect: the American government was outraged, and the American people were worked into a frenzy. Carranza was back in power by this time and took no steps to assuage the fears of the Americans.

In 1916, Huerta was secreted into the United States by the Germans. A few months later, he boarded a train bound for Texas where he planned to slip into Mexico and take over the government there with German support. The Americans found out about this, intercepted his train, and imprisoned Huerta at Ft. Bliss, Texas. The immediate response from Mexico created a diplomatic nightmare: the Americans had imprisoned the deposed head of a foreign government, and now Mexico was crying "foul!" But this simple act relieved the Germans of having to figure out who to deal with in Mexico. It was Carranza, the same leader with whom the Americans were dealing.

The Germans then stepped up their efforts to persuade Mexico to go to war with the United States, which would keep the Americans out of Europe. The U.S.A. at that time was not capable of fighting a war on two fronts. In fact, it was not ready to fight anywhere due to the pacifist policies of Woodrow Wilson who steadfastly avoided all paths leading to conflict. Wilson was just as much confused by the changing leadership of Mexico as the Germans were. The only difference being that Germany did not care who was in power, and the United States had every reason to find someone friendly with whom to deal.

Even though the American fear of a Mexican alliance with Japan was ongoing, nothing ever came of it. Japan, for her part, continued to rattle the cage throughout 1916[3]. At the same time Germany began a direct appeal to Carranza, who was listening. The Germans proposed that if Mexico were to declare war on the United States and should the Axis powers win in Europe, that the Mexicans would recover all of the territory once part of Mexico which had been annexed by the United States. That is, Texas, New Mexico, California, Arizona, and part of Nevada would at once be ceded to Mexico at the cessation of hostilities. In addition, Mexico would be paid several million reichmarks for her help. It was a tempting offer.

No one knows if Carranza was actually considering the deal. He neither accepted nor turned down the offer, and throughout the last half of 1916, the Germans were actively seeking his acceptance. The author of the most potent message was Germany's foreign secretary to the United States, Arthur Zimmerman, who was as popular in America as in his homeland. From his embassy suite in New York, Zimmerman continued courting the American government and the public while making overtures to Mexico. This was the situation in the summer of 1916 at the time of the Carrizal Affair.

Upon returning to Germany, Zimmerman decided to put the offer to the Mexicans in writing. The Allies had cut all German undersea telegraph cables early in the war. Cleverly, Zimmerman had found a source by which he could send diplomatic messages—by using the telegraph in the United States embassy in Berlin. Since the United States was not at war at the time, it still had an ambassador there. These messages were routed through Washington, unread by the Americans, and sent on to Carranza.

The British were listening, though, and successfully decoded the messages. Notified by their diplomatic channels so as not to give away the manner in which it was decoded, Wilson was furious—finally. When confronted by this news, the darling of American society, Zimmerman admitted the overture, shortly after February 1, 1917, the date of resumption of unrestricted warfare. All the pressure of the past three years now came to a head, and war with Germany was inevitable.

---

[3]   A couple of years later, just before the Americans declared war, the Japanese affirmed their loyalty to the Allies and the United States.

History books will say that the resumption of submarine warfare finally caused Wilson to act, but if that is the case it is a mystery as to why he waited until April 2, 1917, to ask for a declaration. The Zimmerman telegram was revealed and admitted in late February and again in March that year so it would seem that once again the pacifist Wilson was looking for a way around the U-boat problem when the Zimmerman telegram came to light.

One other theory has been put forth as to why the Wilson finally asked for a declaration of war: For three years he had imagined himself as the savior of the civilized world in which he would negotiate a peace among the belligerents. After Germany's declaration of February 1, the Zimmerman telegram, and all the prior acts of the central powers were added up, plus the fact that France and Britain had little regard for his passiveness, Wilson may have finally realized that to become the "great arbitrator," he must commit the United States to be a part of the conflict. That is, until the Americans were "blooded," she would have no right to participate in peace negotiations.

All of these are interesting theories, and it is possible that the beginning of the involvement of America in the European conflict was a combination of all those factors.

CHAPTER FOUR

WAR WITH MEXICO?

~~~~

With more than 5,000 population Thomasville is entitled to general free delivery of mail, but we have not provided safe walks for the delivery men, and therefore we must continue as before.—The Dispatch, *Thomasville Department, August 9, 1916*

~~~~

On June 19, 1916, Wilson finally called up the National Guard to be ready to invade Mexico if necessary. Captain Newby, Captain Leonard, and the other commanders of the Third Brigade were notified to have their troops ready to march by noon that day. Orders for where they were headed and when would come later, but the excitement generated was electric. The men truly felt like they were headed to war with Mexico and that they would be seeing action soon.

Civilians were no less excited. The local chapter of the Confederate veterans cheered the men with patriotic fervor. Businesses and individuals feted the soldiers throughout their wait for definitive orders, and the ladies of the town provided everything from food to clothing for the soon-to-be heroes.

One of the young men who answered the call to enlist was Marvin Lambeth, a young lad only nineteen years old from Trinity where the two counties, Davidson and Randolph, share a border. He also worked at a local chair factory, and so Thomasville was essentially his hometown. It is thought that he joined during this time as patriotic fervor swept the country. He was medium height and slight build, not a very imposing young warrior, but a nice young man eager to do his duty. His older brother was seriously ill with tuberculosis and lived a tent outside the house because it was thought that fresh air was the best cure for the disease.

Very soon after being notified, the Blues did receive orders to entrain for Camp Glenn for further training and deployment. On Friday evening, June 22, between two and three thousand people assembled on the square in Thomasville to wish the boys well as they departed for the coast. The band from Farmer played, patriotic songs were sung, and speeches were made, most notably by Cameron Morrison, future governor, senator, and representative from Charlotte. Barbecued lamb and pig were served to all, and a New Testament was presented to the members of the military company, whereupon the boys themselves ascended the flowered platform and sang several patriotic songs.

On the morning of Saturday, July 23, 1916, members of Company L in Thomasville and Company A in Lexington assembled at their respective railway stations for transport to Camp Glenn. A huge gathering of well-wishers sent them off in fine style. One enthusiastic northerner took Captain Leonard's hand and said, "I wasn't born in North Carolina, but it wasn't my fault. I want to congratulate you on your splendid spirit and wish you good luck." A young man from Salisbury volunteered for service at the station and was assigned to Company A immediately.

There had also been some desertions. Two well-known Davidson boys (names withheld) were members of Company A but went into hiding when the guard was called up. The father of one, uncle to the other, convinced them of the error of their ways. He then persuaded Captain Leonard to take them back as he said they had acted out of fear of the unknown rather than cowardice. They were among the boys who boarded the train for Camp Glenn. Other desertions or draft-dodging cases were much more serious and involved some infamous families in the county.

As the train pulled out from Lexington and then Thomasville, well-wishers cheered and waved as the train disappeared northeastward. After a stop in Greensboro to pick up a few more men, the troop train wound its way east to Raleigh then southeast to the coast. Soon the rolling hills of the Piedmont gave way to the flatter coastal plain, familiar territory to all but a few of the men. Upon arrival, the troops immediately began pioneer duty since the camp was not large enough to take all these men at once. For the summer camps, they had come a few companies at a time, so the camp was enlarged to accommodate the increased numbers. This probably involved only pitching more tents and adding a few buildings. The camp quickly settled into a familiar routine, only this time, more than one week would pass with no deployment home.

National Guard troops from other states were already on their way to the border. Those from New Mexico and Texas had been called up immediately. The plan was for several brigades at a time to post on the border, perhaps one hundred thousand or more men at any one time. It was anybody's guess as to how these men were to be used, but they were to await orders to invade Mexico at a moment's notice. The administration fervently hoped that would not be the case. In fact, General Pershing, being regular army, was disdainful of the National Guardsmen. Meanwhile, the North Carolina boys trained daily at Camp Glenn.

Sometime in the summer or autumn of 1916, the war department in Washington issued posters depicting scenes of the military and of Mexican peasants during the crisis. The poster was probably issued either before deployment or shortly after. Printed by the government with a blank rectangle in the center, it was a simple matter for the local printer to add the names of the individual National Guard unit. This poster is the only reliable complete listing found in months of research of Company L as they went to Texas. The poster is in the possession of the author.

Captain Carleton H. Newby, Commander
1ˢᵗ Lieut. Wallace B. Stone   **2ⁿᵈ Lieut. Robert O. Little**
First Sergt. Daniel C. Culbreth
Supply Sergt. Robert B. Talbert   **Mess Sergt.** Paul Green

Sergeants	Corporals	Mechanic
Reuben J. Westmoreland	Charlie W. Harrison	Sam. A. Myers
Joseph M. White	Willie R. Westmoreland	**Buglers**
Milton W. Veach	John A. Stratton	Thomas O. Ragan
Lorenzo D. Player	George C. Jones	Ernest A. Davis
Ernest M. Batten	John D. Beck	**Cooks**
		Henley C. Culbreth
		Clarence H. Harris

Privates	Privates	Privates
David B. Barkley	Oliver C. Herman	Golden C. Presley
John H. Burris	William H. Hulin	Dolph A. Poole
James S. Burton	Frank Hoke	Wiley Spencer
George C. Brown	Wiley R. Howell	Charlie Sluder

George W. Broadway	*Charlie Hicks*	*Willey S. Sanders*
Henry H. Boger	*Loyd C. Irvin*	*Arthur R. Swaim*
Fritts E. Creekman	*Spaight Laughlin*	*Albert W. Waisner*
Chester G. Coltrane	*Emmett. H. Leonard*	*James W. Winslow*
Fred H. Craver	*William F. McGee*	*Lewis H. Welborn*
Hobson F. Fraylick	*Charlie D. Mendenhall*	*Edgar L. Wood*
James R. Fletcher	*Jesse Mann*	*Iradell D. Yarborough*
	Robah P. Osborne	

Wallace Stone had been the bugler in 1910, but by 1916 had risen to the rank of first lieutenant. Born in 1891 he was only nineteen when he joined the Blues. He was an ambitious young man, looking to make his mark in the world.

Recruiting for more men was ongoing from call-up to entrainment. Those who signed up for Company A, about thirty in number, were sent with the others to camp. Within a few weeks, thirty-two men from Company A were sent home for one reason or another, mostly for being underweight. Some of the original members received a family exemption, which, it seemed, could be had for the asking. A few had severe dental problems. Presumably they were sent home to get their conditions corrected. No record was found as to whether they reenlisted and returned to camp.

Captain Leonard and Lieutenant Cecil from Company A were home, recruiting more men in Davidson and Rowan counties. Although outwardly optimistic, both Leonard and Captain Newby were disappointed at the small number of men who were volunteering. There was no conscription law at the time, so enlistments were wholly dependent on volunteers.

The Thomasville Company reportedly had ninety-two men eventually. (The list above shows only fifty-three.) Notably absent from the roster are W. O. Burgin, who had resigned and moved to Greensboro; A. H. Ragan, who had resigned and was a judge in recorder's court; and Zed Griffith, who was then mayor of Thomasville. Only six men from Company L returned from Camp Glenn with family exemptions.

The location of the troops at Glenn was a very fortunate turn of events for the hometown boys since they were easily able to take leave and return home occasionally. A reporter visiting the camp in August found the men to be happy and healthy, desiring to get into the fight in Mexico, if there was to be one. Lieutenant Stone was on his honeymoon at this time and not in camp. The last days in camp were very busy, but Lieutenant Little did take a leave to return home for the birth of his fourth son, Max E. Little, on September 18, 1916.

The daily routine of drilling, marching, and target practice was finally ended September 28, 1916, when the Third Brigade was loaded on Pullman cars for the trip southwestward to Camp Stewart, on the site of Ft. Bliss near El Paso, Texas. The path of the trains was well publicized being routed through Raleigh, Charlotte, Atlanta, Birmingham, Memphis, Texarkana, and El Paso. All along the way, civilians turned out to cheer the boys on. In Atlanta, they took a swim in the Y.M.C.A. swimming pool.

The first "wet" stop was Fort Worth, Texas—the only alcoholic beverage available at home was moonshine, which was plentiful but illegal. The Easterners must have enjoyed the interlude there because several were inadvertently left behind when the train pulled out. One boy from Company K, thinking he was in High Point, walked off the back of the train, sustaining minor injuries. All those left behind caught later trains including the injured soldier and were a few hours or maybe a day behind the main body.

Cooking was done in the baggage cars. The various cities along the way were all welcome stops for all the boys. The Red Cross met the troops at every station, providing food and a place to bathe. Memphis, Tennessee, was the favorite stop along the route. In all, the trip lasted for five days and required ten trains, with the troops finally arriving in El Paso on October 2, 1916.

When the Davidson County boys finally arrived at El Paso, the Philadelphia troops who were supposed to have left had not. This meant that the North Carolinians had to camp further out than planned, pitching tents where none had been before. The pyramid tents used generally had wooden floor boards, making life easier for the eight occupants. Since the Philadelphians had not gone home as yet, the North Carolina boys pitched their tents with no floors. Once the northern boys moved out, the Southerners were able to move in to prepared areas.

The Southerners got along very well with their northern counterparts. On the day the Philadelphians moved out, they were serenaded by their German-American band, and the Southerners gave a mighty shout, whereupon the band struck up "Dixie" in salute to the North Carolinians.

For years this picture (above) has been identified as Third Brigade Troops in Raleigh-1918, but the Third Brigade had ceased to exist by that time. While it does show the brigade on the capitol grounds, it is unlikely that it was in 1918. Notice that the rifles are in "stack arms," and the whole scene is very casual with a few ladies and gentlemen around, which was not the case in 1918 as the troops hurried northward for transport to France. More likely, this is in 1916 on their way to Camp Glenn. (Courtesy: North Carolina Archives). Below, Company L unloads on their first day at Camp Stewart, R. O. Little supervising. (Courtesy: Patsy Henderson)

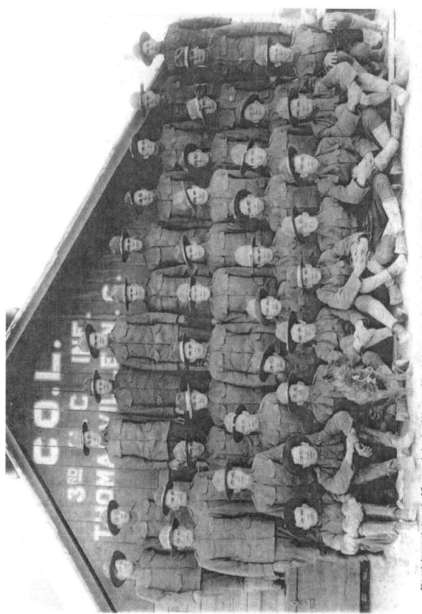

The only known photograph of Company L showing thirty-nine of the ninety-two men who went to Camp Stewart, TX in 1916. Capt. Carl Newby is seated second from left; 1st Lt. Wallace Stone with the dog; Lt. R.O. Little is standing at left on second row. Others are unidentified.

Soon the camp settled in to a routine with lots of marching and exercise to keep the boys busy. One early account of camp life by Major Wade Phillips is as follows:

About ten a.m. the wind began to blow and the dust storms to rise. One soldier here says he met a man who told him it rained here last year and I heard of another native who prophesied rain next summer. So the dust came in storms, in clouds, it drifted dust, rained dust, dust came up from the earth and returned from the sky; often we could not see and in the wind could not hear. For several days we ate dust, talked dust, our thoughts were dusty, we slept in dust, had dust in our clothes, pockets, shoes. The whole camp seven miles long by fourteen wide was one huge ocean of dust. Then the men . . . began to droop, and their enthusiasm began to fail. They had left the mosquitoes of Morehead to be choked to death on fine dry clouds. However, even the **dust** *had its bright side. For instance under the fierce sun, it is perfectly sterile. You can hang out your clothes in it, then beat them good and they are cleaner than by laundry. It is gentle dust. It will crawl into your tent, onto your cot, under your blanket and in your eyes, and if you say anything a puff of wind will blow your blanket away and cover you in dirt. It is manufactured by army trucks and mule wagons. There is none at El Paso or out of camp. We are now getting used to it. No one is expected to stay clean. This also helps some.* (Letter to *The Dispatch* from Major Phillips, October 18, 1916.)

Eventually it did rain and when it did, it rained hard which made the men prefer the dust. Up to five inches fell at one time, creating torrents of water which flowed through the camp, making lakes out of low places. Some of the tents were completely surrounded by water, and men had to be rescued. Then the sun came out and quickly evaporated the water but left the ground hard so that very soon the dust was choking them again. No evidence remained that it had rained except for gullies and wagon tracks made in the mire, now hardened, producing more dust.

Company L's permanent campsite was located on the Rio Grande, about five miles from El Paso where the two railroads cross the Rio Grande near a cement plant. Company K was nearby. This was not far from a smelter owned by the Guggenheims whose furnaces extracted silver and gold twenty-four hours per day, making for a beautiful red glow after dark. Company A had the accommodations located on the site of old Ft. Bliss, and Company L was located at the railroad trestle near the smelter. The cement plant and smelter provided electricity and baths (which many of the men did not have at home) for the military camp, making it fairly pleasant for the guardsmen.

There are always towns that spring up near army camps, but El Paso was already thriving before the military arrived and was not dependent on the soldiers as some military towns were. In other words, the town was ready for the soldiers. It was only five miles away and there were trolleys and streetcars running right up to the camp from the town. Already in place were movie houses (silent movies since talkies were thirteen years in the future), saloons, gambling casinos, and almost every distraction a soldier could want. The accounts hastened to add that the wives and sweethearts had no need to worry because the men were remaining mostly temperate and celibate.

It wasn't all pleasant, though. The camp was right next to the river, and the men sometimes became jumpy at any sound from the south side. John MacDonald and Norman Smith from the Lexington Company on guard duty heard sounds in the river and shouted a challenge three times with no response. With their rifles at the ready, their eyes slowly adjusted to the darkness as a figure fell prostrate on the bank of the river. They finally determined that it was local man who had had too much to drink, leading his horse across, whereupon he was arrested and taken before the captain of the guard. He never knew how close he came to being shot.

Another hazard was more serious as detailed in a letter from Major Phillips, commander of the Third Brigade. It seems that at this time of the year, shoals of poisonous snakes, probably water moccasins, come up from the river seeking warmth. The warmest place happened to be the tents of the National Guardsmen who had to beat the reptiles off with clubs and whatever else they could find.

About a month after their arrival, several changes were made affecting both companies A and L. Sergeant Major Luther Propst of A was promoted to regimental sergeant major with John Thompson taking his place at company level. (Propst had disappeared one Sunday and when he turned up later, he claimed he had been into Mexico. No one doubted it.) In L, 1st Lt. Wallace Stone and Pvt. Arthur Swaim were sent to brigade HQ. Also, First Sergeant Dan Culbreth had an attack of appendicitis and underwent a successful operation. He was recovering nicely, according to the reports.

On November 7, 1916, the general election for president of the United States was held. Charles Evans Hughes and President Wilson were the two main candidates, and the latter pledged to keep the country out of the European conflict. "He kept us out of war!" was one of the campaign slogans. Many in the southwest supported Hughes, but when the votes were tallied Wilson had won reelection. Torchlight parades were held in El Paso, celebrating the victory with Captain Leonard and other guardsmen in the front of the procession. It was very unmilitary and against regulations, but they did not seem to care. Major Phillips had characterized Leonard as a "live wire" in one letter to The Dispatch.

Judging from the accounts, it seems that guard duty along the Rio Grande was a shared duty. The North Carolinians were to guard a section of the border about fifty miles long from El Paso west to Las Cruces. Company A's duty station was at old Ft. Bliss, Company K at Sylvester, and Company L at the Cement Plant, all located along the Rio Grande River. Companies and brigades would rotate duty along its banks in order to sound the alarm should hostilities arise. It also meant a lot of downtime for all the boys when not on guard duty. Carranza's men were within view on the other side of the river, and both armies kept a watchful eye on the other, each guarding against incursion by the other. Orders for both armies, Mexican and American, were to keep the other from crossing the river. After Company A was augmented by Company C, Carranza's numbers also increased opposite them.

Like most soldiers, many liked to sleep in, so it was ordered that before breakfast at the sound of the bugle, the men would turn out and run a couple of miles. This conditioning was modeled after the training in the German army.

Most of the days in camp were filled with the same old army routine—drilling and marching, marching and drilling—but occasionally there were maneuvers and sham battles. There's one such time the brigades were divided up, the North Carolinians on one side and the Pennsylvanians on the other, for a two-day contest. (The Philadelphians had gone home but the Thirteenth Pennsylvania remained.) The Southern boys were victorious on the first day but lost on the second when they vainly assaulted a strong point held by the northerners. Apparently the battle was pretty real as several of the combatants from both sides came to blows and had to be separated by cooler heads.

A rumor of a hundred-mile hike proved to be false, but there were plenty of shorter treks through the countryside. The mountains were only a few miles from camp and many days the men marched there and back. These were the southern tip of the Rocky Mountains, which at this point, were not very high. Still, a lot of sore limbs and aching feet resulted from these excursions. Meals were taken out in the open with rations carried along by each man. These hikes served to strengthen the men and keep them active since boredom is the devil's workshop.

At Camp Stewart, El Paso, TX. Above: Bruce T???, H.C. Culbreth, C. H. Newby, Daniel C. Culbreth, John Beck. Below: W. S. Saunders, J. S. Burton, R. J. Westmoreland, Sam Myers, H. C. Culbreth. (Both Courtesy: Patsy Henderson.)

Above left: On maneuvers outside Camp Stewart, C. H. Newby with arms folded facing camera; Right: R. O. Little and C. H. Newby; Below: W. H. Hulin, H. F. Fraylick, W. R. Howell, C. G. Coltrane and G. C. Brown take a break.
(All Courtesy: Patsy Henderson)

Site of the encampment of Company L on the Rio Grande. The El Paso and Southwest Railroad (1) and the Southern Pacific Railroad (2) cross the river at this point. The cement plant be seen under the railroad trestle at left center. (Courtesy: Patsy Henderson)

An lone sentinel (center, left) keeps watch on the banks of the Rio Grande River, ready to sound the alarm should any incursions occur. The embankment is made of mud and sticks. (Courtesy: NC State Archives, Col. J. Van B. Metts Collection)

The excitement of the first few days in camp had worn off by the second or third week, and the men found many ways to entertain themselves. Aside from the trips to El Paso, boxing matches were held for the enjoyment of the men. The lightweight champion of the world, Willie Ritchie, gave exhibitions and was well liked by all the guardsmen. Inter-regimental bouts were also held on a regular basis. The arena was over at Camp Cotton across the state line in New Mexico since boxing was illegal in Texas. The arena, outdoors probably, seated five thousand men.

Occasionally there were cowboy exhibitions at a permanent arena outside El Paso. Local cowhands would ride, rope, and shoot Wild West style much to the enjoyment of those attending. These events were the forerunner of modern-day rodeos.

Often there were contests of a different kind—singing. After "The Star-Spangled Banner" was sung by all, the men from each state would stand and sing a favorite song. Massachusetts, New Jersey, Ohio, Pennsylvania, North Carolina, South Carolina, and many other states competed to see who could sing the best and the loudest. South Carolina and Massachusetts generally won the loudest competition. After all the songs were sung, they always finished the songfest by singing together:

> No North, no South today,
> No more boys in Blue and Gray.

Such was the camaraderie of the men who shared this time together.

Another form of entertainment involved the local fauna. Animals the men had never seen before were abundant outside camp, especially jack rabbits. Burros, gopher rats, rattlesnakes, and prairie dogs were there too, but the fascination was with the long-eared creatures. It was great sport to shoot some for food, but the greatest sport was to actually catch them by hand. One Pennsylvania guardsman, in admiration after losing a sham battle to the Tar Heels said, "Thunder! What do you expect? Those blame fellows march twenty miles, fight a battle, and then catch jack rabbits all the way back!"

After getting everything in order and not knowing what to expect, the men were naturally eager to get into the fight. Pershing was just over the border somewhere, and daily the National Guardsmen could see Mexicans across the narrow and sometimes shallow river. Carranza's men could be seen easily, but the Mexicans had no uniforms or even similar equipment, so it was impossible to distinguish Carranza's men from Villa's if there were any.

Before the arrival of the North Carolinians, some of the Kentucky boys did fire when a Mexican across the river unwisely picked that time and place to light a cigarette. Thinking it was the flash of artillery fire, the Kentuckians let loose with about 1,400 rounds of machine gun lead. There was no report of any casualties. The Kentuckians, before their departure earlier that summer, citing some knowledge of the Carolinians' history, claimed that when the Tar Heels arrived, war would surely break out since the North Carolina boys were such scrappers.

The rumor mill was also very active. "Latrine news" had Pancho Villa on the attack at Juarez across the Rio Grande and a few weeks earlier in the Texas town of Tobin. Another story said that the bandit had raided Ft. Bliss nearby and had stolen over three thousand horses. He was everywhere and nowhere at the same time, but for the first few weeks in camp, these rumors kept the guardsmen on their toes.

There was some excitement for the Davidson boys also. One night in the early part of 1917, Ralph Myers from Company A, while on guard duty, thought he saw something and ran to tell Captain Leonard that two hundred Mexican bandits were crossing the Rio Grande at that moment. The captain and his executive officer, Lt. Joe Cecil, quickly grabbed weapons and ammunition and took off for the river at a dead run. Upon arrival, they found three Mexicans peacefully watering their horses in the shallow river. Whether there ever were more than these three or just the imagination of an excitable young man is anybody's guess.

And Company A did exchange shots with some Mexicans across the river on one occasion. A copse of trees commonly called the "peace grove" was a source of trouble sometimes, and one night several shots rang out from it directed at the Lexington men. Company A answered with about one hundred rounds of their own whereupon the grove grew quiet, cigarettes were extinguished, and nothing more was heard from that direction for the rest of the encampment. Captain Leonard doubted that anyone was injured during the incident.

Other incidents were more humorous than serious. Since Company A was camped near the abandoned buildings of old Ft. Bliss, guard duty was something of an adventure in itself. The old foundations and crumbling walls made for odd sounds. Owls and other night creatures added to the creepy noises during the night hours, and many a boy on patrol around these structures thought he saw and heard things that may not have been there. Several rounds were expended at phantom noises among the shadows, and many stories were told in later years about this particular detail.

It was no less creepy in the open areas. During daylight hours, the saguaro cactus appeared to shimmer in the heat, but at night the imagination would run wild as this large plant with the upright branches positively appeared to move. The more a guard stared at it, the more it seemed to move to the left or right and even forward. Many an innocent saguaro cactus was filled with lead as it seemed ready to infiltrate the camp in spite of all attempts to stop it. Morning would bring laughter and relief to the troopers.

Homesickness was a common feeling from all the boys as in all military encampments. The feeling was that if they were not going to fight, they might as well go home; just do one or the other. Initially the rumor mill had the men going into Mexico the next day or the next, but Pershing had little confidence in the militia as he called the National Guardsmen and would not let that happen[4], so talk of home became the most common activity. Officers were eventually strictly forbidden to speak about orders home and were challenged to come up with new ways to keep the men active. Letters from loved ones always cheered the men and were eagerly anticipated. "You should see the men brighten up," Major Phillips wrote. "The soldiers crowd about. One gets three letters, another a card for illustration, and then a soldier very anxious and expectant gets none at all. I have watched those, how they stooped forward in dejection and slowly went back to their tents completely and utterly disappointed. It almost brings tears to the eyes of a hardened soldier."

Major Phillips, in another letter to *The Dispatch*, told of one member of Company K, a Private Auman, who was detailed to light the morning fire in the incinerator (probably an old metal barrel) which was used to consume all the combustibles produced by the encampment. It happened to be pouring rain at the time, and he had a lot of difficulty getting a spark in order to make a flame. Finally he did get it started and added more paper and wood to the fire. As he continued to add fuel, he slipped in the mud, causing both feet to slide

---

[4] Pershing had stated, "To attempt to put dependence upon the militia is absolutely absurd and ridiculous." *Borrowed Soldiers* by Mitchell Yockelson, 2008, University of Oklahoma Press: Norman, p. 4. In general, a militia is an untrained force gathered at the last moment before an enemy strikes to defend a hometown or facility. This description does not fit the well-trained National Guardsmen.

against the incinerator, knocking it over, extinguishing the fire, and covering his uniform with muck. Auman's sentiments were shared by most of the men by this time as he rose to his feet and shouted to the heavens, "I WANT TO GO HOME!"

Spirits were always lifted on payday, however, and the men were paid in gold coin. The most prevalent rumor as to why gold was used was that the paper script had been picked up by a whirlwind one day and $20,000 was scattered across the sand for a mile. After that the paymaster insisted on the heavier currency. Another rumor was that Villa himself wanted to buy machine guns on the black market, and the only source for them was Camp Stewart. Since he was rumored to be offering gold, the U.S. paid in kind to keep the temptation away from the soldiers. Not until the beginning of the war was the amount paid for the soldiers discussed in the news, but judging from an article almost a year after the expedition a good guess is that privates were paid about $30 per month, although no definite accounting was found.

The Young Men's Christian Association, the YMCA, was in camp throughout the entire time any troops were on the border. The organization in this capacity was the forerunner of the USO and generally set up their facility wherever the soldiers went. There the men could obtain many personal items such as soap or toothbrushes and could either write or dictate letters to loved ones at home. There are many examples of letters written using paper with the YMCA logo. Their tent or building was always crowded and served a much-needed role. Throughout the encampment, the YMCA was a place where officers and men could go to relax, see old friends, and write home.

It was not as hot as it had been when they arrived in camp, at least not at night. Shortly after arrival, the men were issued stoves for heating and overcoats to keep warm. At night, the thermometer would plunge below freezing, so water for shaving was solid ice when the men awoke, but by noon they were in shirtsleeves again. Since they were only issued two sets of clothing, many of the boys wore overalls to protect the uniforms from nicks and tears. Officers, of course, paid for their own uniforms. Some of the officers, including R. O., built small huts which cost as much as $4.50 to build. This activity also kept the men busy and their minds occupied.

Christmas on the border was observed as well as possible. Makeshift Christmas trees and ornaments were displayed, and small gifts were exchanged. Some packages arrived from home, and the men grew even more homesick. Since the military did not supply anything other than normal rations, many of the

Above: Scene from Fort Stewart, Texas, 1917.(Courtesy of Lena Little) Below: The Y.M.C.A. was ever present and a welcome place where men could relax, buy snacks and write home. (Courtesy: Patsy Henderson)

companies pooled their money in order to have a special meal for Christmas. Company I was typical which with the captain's permission bought turkey and all the trimmings for the men. Tables were pushed together to form one long one, and a blessing was asked, but as they sat down to the holiday feast, the wind came up and whipped up the fine sand. The men covered the food as best they could, but it was too late—the sand had worked its way onto every inch of the food, and it was ruined. The fellows ate what they could of it, but it was not very appetizing, and they eventually went out and bought supper in town.

Wade Phillips, ever the author, penned the following:

CHRISTMAS ON THE BORDER

> *The crescent moon swings low o'er the Rio Grande,*
> *Giant mountains gleam along the edge of night;*
> *Myriad campfires glow throughout the desert land,*
> *While above the tented plains there streams the light*
> *Of Christmas stars. Here wails the warrior band*
> *From the old North State, who loyal to the right,*
> *Answered with patriot zeal their country's call,*
> *Willing to yield their lives for peace and all.*
> *But not for them the glory of victories won*
> *In battle, nor the joy of redressing wrong;*
> *A task more trying, with no fight begun,*
> *To toil and train in exile, while they long*
> *For hearts at home, not knowing that duty done*
> *Aright will lift their souls and make them strong.*
> *Service alone makes dear our land. For those who prove*
> *By waiting and serving are opened new doors of love.*
> *Camp Stewart W. H. P.*
> *El Paso, Texas.*

It had to end eventually. As detailed in chapter 4, Pershing never did catch Villa, never even saw him. The "punitive" expedition ended on February 7, 1917, when the army returned to the United States at El Paso, Texas. Newsreel photographers were there to capture the dramatic event as Pershing and his staff rode into Camp Stewart amid the cheers of thousands of National Guardsmen, and the New Mexico National Guard fired a thirteen-gun salute with their artillery. The army then paraded through the streets of El Paso, where the civilian population added their accolades.

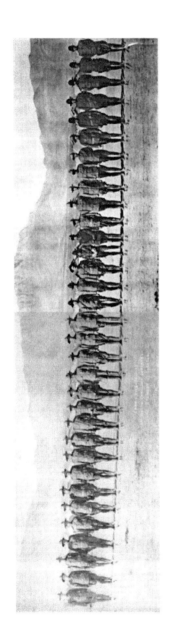
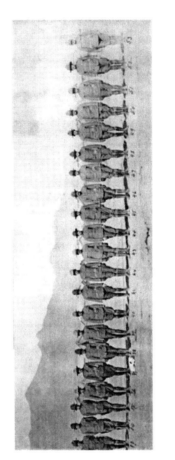

Officers of the 3rd North Carolina Regiment at Camp Stewart, 1916

Undoubtedly, many of those men in the newsreel were North Carolina's finest. Among them was R. O. with his camera who snapped two photographs of Pershing as he crossed onto U.S. soil. For the experience gained, Pershing declared the mission a complete success, and it would be many years before any feeling of failure would surface. After all, events in Germany would quickly overshadow this part of American history.

As the regular army marched back into Texas, their destination was their army camp—Ft. Bliss nearby. Passes and furloughs would be provided to them, but it would be more than a month before the North Carolinians and Pennsylvanians were ordered home. After all, Pancho Villa and his gang were still out there . . . somewhere.

After the army's return to American soil, Villa moved in and reoccupied the territory just vacated. The area south of the border with Texas once again was in his hands, and he was considered a hero by the people there.

Hostilities did not end in 1917. Tensions along the border remained high. In August 1918 at a border crossing near Nogales, Arizona, a Mexican official apparently admitted a countryman to which the Americans objected. Guns were pulled by the Americans which were met with hundreds more from the Mexican side. The ensuing battle resulted in the death of three American troops and twenty-eight wounded. Mexican casualties were estimated at between 100 to 150. President Carranza sent a personal envoy to Nogales to express regret over the incident.

Even as late as June 28, 1919, American troops crossed into Mexico in answer to threats from the Mexicans, reportedly sent by Villa. The Ninety-second Artillery Brigade crossed the river near Juarez in to Mexico on that night and a short battle ensued as Americans fired while standing in water up to their knees. Mexican prisoners were taken to Ft. Bliss and a herd of horses corralled nearby.

Villa remained entrenched in Mexican politics and forged a truce with Carranza in 1919. In 1920, Carranza himself was assassinated, and Huerta took over as president. Villa retired to his villa in the Chihuahua province and received a government pension for himself and some of his men. On July 20, 1923, he was assassinated in the town of Parral by a group of seven Mexicans. One of the assassins was killed and the rest captured, but only two were imprisoned and just for a couple of months. No clear motive for the murder was ever established.

General Pershing as he entered Camp Stewart from Mexico after
the "punitive expedition" into Mexico, February 7, 1917.
(Photos by R. O. Little, Courtesy: Patsy Henderson)

The Texas and New Mexico National Guards as well as a regular army artillery brigade remained on the border until after the war, guarding against any incursion by Mexicans. Since these remaining units were stationed there, their service was rewarded by the authorization after the World War to wear a silver chevron similar to the gold chevron which was indicative of overseas service.

CHAPTER FIVE

HOME, THEN WHAT?

Once Pershing returned to the United States, there was no longer a pressing need to keep most of the National Guard on the border. The Texas units and a few others, who had been there since the beginning of hostilities, would remain; but the bulk of the troops were getting ready to head home to an uncertain future. As discussed earlier, the Germans had virtually declared war on the United States, by resuming unrestricted submarine warfare on February 1, 1917. However, Wilson once again stalled and sent protests to the Germans. This time he even recalled the American ambassador, but still he did not ask for war. He delayed even though the press, the Congress, and the general public knew the inevitability of our entry into the heretofore European war.

Then there was the most provocative of these overtures, referenced in chapter 3, the telegram detailing the German offer to Carranza and the Mexicans. Would the Mexicans accept? After all, Pershing had been deep into Mexican territory, relations had been in the cellar for several years; the Tampico Affair, the battle and occupancy of Vera Cruz battle, and the Carrizal Affair were all hot issues. No acceptance or refusal of the proposal ever came from Mexico. The reasons for the silence are open to speculation.

As the National Guardsmen prepared to go home, rumors were rife about what was going to happen. Newspapers opined that they would be used in home guard duty, while the regular army would go to France. Since U-boats had been sinking ships off the Atlantic, just off the American coast, many thought the boys may be stationed at coastal facilities like Camp Glenn and perform similar duties to the one they had just finished. Almost no one realized what was finally to happen.

By the end of February 1917 the boys were still in Texas and were ready to go home awaiting transport when a tragedy occurred to Company A. Childhood diseases had been sweeping the camp, not an epidemic, but enough to keep the doctors busy. A popular member of that unit, Corporal Willis Vestal Wilson, died suddenly as a result of an attack of mumps. Death came within two weeks of the departure for home of the rest of Company A. After a funeral service which was attended by the whole regiment, his body was shipped home to his grieving family. A few months before, in December 1916, a Sgt. Everette T. Lawrence, Company A from Seagrove, had also died after an illness lasting eight days. There were no reported casualties for Company L while guarding the Mexican border.

Finally, on March 17, the boys started home, but by then the certainty of war caused great uncertainty as to their destination. Many National Guard units from other states had already reached their home station, and those units were mustered out. As they crossed into the Old North State, their elation was tempered by the department's announcement that the National Guard, then in transit, would proceed to designated destinations and would not muster out. Those that had already reached their home stations would be recalled.

By the narrowest of margins, fifteen minutes by one account, the orders to keep the Third North Carolina Brigade in federal service were late in coming. The boys passed through Raleigh, were mustered out, and sent home, before those orders were issued. The Second Brigade was not as fortunate and went into bivouac near Goldsboro.

And so it was that the two Davidson County units and all the rest of the Third Brigade were able to come home. The crowds that welcomed them on March 27 were huge even though delays caused the trains to arrive well after dark. The train from Raleigh let the Thomasville boys off about 10:00 p.m. and the Lexington troops about 10:30 p.m. Bands played and speeches were made, but the boys were only anxious to see their loved ones for the first time in many months. The following night, the townspeople turned out for an official welcome home.

The reverie was not to last, however. Everyone knew that the orders had been cut and that the Third would be recalled; they just did not know when. Even at this late date, the ultimate use of the guardsmen had not been announced. Many still clung to the hope that they would be used for coastal duty or to guard bridges, factories, and cities. Any hint of the possibility that they would be shipped overseas was absent from the newspapers and correspondence.

~~~~~

On April 2, 1917, President Wilson addressed a joint session of Congress, asking for a declaration of war against Germany. On April 6, 1917, the Congress responded:

> Whereas, the recent course of the Imperial German government is in fact nothing less than war against the government and people of the United States:
>
> Resolved by the senate and house of representatives of the United States, in Congress assembled;
>
> That the state of belligerency between the United States and the Imperial German government which has thus been thrust upon the United States is hereby formally declared; and
>
> That the President be, and he is hereby, authorized to take immediate steps not only to put the country in thorough state of defense but also to exert all of its power and employ all of its resources to carry on the war against the Imperial German government and to bring the conflict to a successful termination.[5]

~~~~~

On April 25, the war department, through the governors of most states, sent an appeal to the home station of each National Guard unit to wit: that almost none of the guard units were up to full strength; that no more units will be authorized until the current ones are fully manned; that the citizens, business and civic organizations of each community should endeavor to recruit men to fill the ranks; that those who did join would be able to serve with their hometown units under their own officers; and "It is earnestly suggested that this matter be given immediate consideration as it is believed it will be to the best interests of your community and to the entire state." The appeal was made by the adjutant general, B. S. Royster. Remarkably, the appeal still held no definite purpose for which the men were being kept in federal service.

~~~~

*The Lexington and Thomasville National Guard Companies want about fifty men each to fill their ranks. Young unmarried men, of sound mind and body, between the ages of 18 and 45, with red blood are desired. The conscript officers will begin the draft in about a month. Now is the last chance to join your home company.—*The Dispatch, *May 2, 1917.*

---

[5] The United States would not declare war on Germany's ally, Austria-Hungary, until December 1917.

CHAPTER SIX

THE THIRTIETH DIVISION

The orders finally came. Once the National Guards of the various states had been mobilized, it became necessary for them to be organized as a fighting unit. Accordingly, on July 18, 1917, the Thirtieth Division was formed from National Guard units in North Carolina, South Carolina, and Tennessee. They were officially called into federal service on July 25, 1917, to begin training at Camp Sevier near Greenville, South Carolina. A few weeks later on August 3, the first official assembly of the Old Hickory Division was marked with ceremony and speeches. Intensive training was next, but the Davidson boys had not yet arrived at Camp Sevier. From this time forward, the National Guardsmen would be referred to as part of the National Army.

~~~~~

Having taken note that the three states represented were closely linked to Andrew Jackson—he was born on the North Carolina/South Carolina border, practiced law in Salisbury, and rose to fame in Tennessee—Don MacRae, from Thomasville, North Carolina, suggested that the nickname of the Thirtieth Division should be the "Old Hickory Division" which was accepted. General Order Number 7 dated March 26, 1918, stated that, "Jackson was one of the most commanding personalities in American History. It is his indomitable fighting qualities, [sic] . . . that this Division will emulate."

There has been a lot of speculation as to how and by whom the patch for the division was designed. It was not generally worn on the uniform until after the war, and many stories about its origins have been proposed. The design consisted of an oval surrounded with blue edging—the O—two vertical and two horizontal blue lines—the H—with three Xs for thirty, all on a maroon field. The patch was placed horizontally, that is, with the oval "O" on its side.

One explanation for the supposed "error" was blamed on a tailor who did not know how to place it, and the mistake was perpetuated. Another possible explanation was that the night before a division inspection shortly after the war, the patches were sewn on by French seamstresses who had no idea how it was to be sewn in place. Next morning, it being too late to correct the error, the inspection took place, and the error became a reality.

The mystery may have been resolved, however, by the discovery in the National Archives of a letter to the *Stars and Stripes* from Major B. Y. Read dated December 16, 1918, which referenced General Order 7 and stated,

> The divisional insignia of the 30th Division was adopted and used on the divisional transport as early as June 1918. Therefore, when G. H. Q. directed, in October, that a distinctive divisional insignia be adopted and worn by all officers and men of the division, this design was submitted to G. H. Q. and approved by the commander in chief. The insignia was personally designed by Major General George W. Read . . . It was suggested to him by the nickname of the division which is "OLD HICKORY." [sic]

A drawing of the insignia within that letter depicted the patch on its side. At the beginning of World War II, years in the future, it would be turned vertically to better depict the "H."

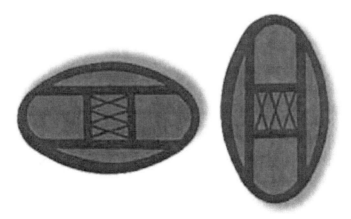

The Old Hickory Patch

WWI   WWII

~~~~~

The newly designated 120th Infantry, the old North Carolina National Guard's Third Brigade, was scheduled to arrive at Camp Sevier on September 2. As had become the custom too many times, the boys from the Piedmont of North Carolina received a rousing send-off from the home folks. By the time the special train arrived in Lexington at 1:00 p.m., Company L and others were already on board and had picked out the best seats. They had even strung a banner along the side of the passenger car, leaving no doubt as to their identity. Burlington's Company I was on board too; and they entertained the crowd with a barber shop quartet, a good one, in addition to one of their own performing a comedy routine. Far from being a sad affair, the send-off was more like a party with everyone laughing and singing, while the boys shook hands with all the young ladies. As the men reboarded the train, shouts of "good-bye and good luck" answered by "we'll be back" filled the festive air.

Scenes such as this repeated themselves throughout the summer of 1917, as the various units, still representing individual towns, arrived at Camp Sevier. Since only a small portion of the land had actually been cleared, the first units assumed pioneer duties. Many hot days and weeks were spent by the first arrivals performing the unsoldierly duties of felling trees, pulling stumps, plowing land, and digging trenches. The site of the camp had been selected partly because of the mild temperatures in the winter months so that the men could train unimpeded by the weather. The Davidson and Randolph boys arrived at Sevier on September 2, 1917, exactly eleven months after their arrival at Camp Stewart, Texas.

It was slow going. Most of the time was spent in setting up areas to accommodate the incoming troops, and little attention was spent on essential training facilities. On October 15, 1917, Major Pratt, the commander of the 105th Engineers, wrote to Secretary of the Navy Josephus Daniels: "Apparently no provision was made to provide rifle ranges and ground for maneuvering troops. It is imperative that our men get the training and rifle practice and use and construction of trenches and machine gun trenches."

The newly formed Thirtieth Division was made up of the following units:

The Fifty-ninth Brigade	*The Sixtieth Brigade*
117th Regiment	119th Regiment
118th Regiment	120th Regiment
114th Machine Gun Battalion	115th Machine gun Battalion
Fifty-fifth Field Artillery Brigade	
113th Field Artillery—75mm guns	114th Field Artillery—75mm guns
115th Field Artillery—155mm	105th Trench Mortar \ Battery Howitzers
Divisional Troops	
113th Machine Gun Battalion	105th Engineer Regiment
105th Field Signal Battalion	Headquarters Troop

Major General Edward M. Lewis was commander of the Old Hickory Division at this time; Brigadier General S. L. Faison commanded the Sixtieth Brigade which was made up of the 119th and 120th Regiments. Some of the old North Carolina First Brigade along with the Tennessee guard became Headquarters and Headquarters Company; others of the old First Brigade were absorbed into the engineer battalion; the old Second Brigade (mostly eastern North Carolinians) became the 119th Infantry; and the old Third Brigade became the 120th Infantry. The commanders down the line were very familiar because they remained virtually the same as before. The old Third Brigade commander was Colonel Sidney Minor who remained as commander of the 120th Regiment, essentially the same position as before; Captains Leonard and Newby remained over their companies as well, and the individual companies retained their letter designation. The units and their commanders at this time were as follows:

First Battalion—Colonel Junious T. Gardner
      Company A, Lexington—Captain James A. Leonard
      Company B, Raleigh—Captain Walter Clark Jr.
      Company C, Henderson—Captain James W. Jenkins
      Company D, Louisburg—Captain Samuel P. Boddie

Second Battalion Colonel Wiley Rodman*
      Company E, Oxford—Captain Elbert E. Fuller
      Company F, Franklinton—Captain James E. Whitfield
      Company G, Reidsville—Captain James H. Mobley
      Company H, Warrenton—Captain Edward C. Price

Third Battalion Major (later Colonel) Wade Phillips
  Company I, Burlington—Captain James C. Freeman
  Company K, Asheboro—Captain Ben F. Dixon
  Company L, Thomasville—Captain Carlton H. Newby
  Company M, Durham—Captain Walter E. Page
  105th Machine Gun Company North Carolina
  —Captain Charles F. Lumsden,
  Supply Company Captain—Stephen E. Winston
  Sanitary Detachment, North Carolina—
  Major Abram R. Winston.

*Colonel Rodman resigned in January 1917 and was succeeded by Lt. Col. J. Van B. Metts who was promoted to colonel.

(There was no Company J in any of the regiments.) This arrangement becomes important in understanding the order of battle. The Headquarters divisional troops (HQ), mostly Tennessee men, were service battalions to all the companies. High Point's Company M of the First Brigade was reformed as the 105th Engineers with Companies A, B, and C. Major (later Colonel) Joseph Hyde Pratt of Chapel Hill was the outstanding commanding officer.

Ben Dixon was in command of Company K by this time. A lawyer living in Raleigh, he was born in Kings Mountain, North Carolina, but his family settled in Gastonia. Dixon was the nearest thing to regular army in the brigade. At age nineteen, he and his identical twin brother, Wright, had enlisted in the army and saw action in the Spanish-American War in 1898-1899. Returning to the United States, he joined the National Guard and went to the border in 1916 where he was promoted to first lieutenant. Upon returning home, he was promoted to captain of Company K. The bond forged between him and his men was a strong one. His residence was Raleigh, and he divided his time between there and Asheboro. His plan was to move his law practice to Asheboro after the imminent war.

CHAPTER SEVEN

DESERTERS

(This is a difficult chapter to write. In fact, it was left out of the first edition of this book due to the sensitive nature of the material. The subject of desertion is never a good one to write about, but it did occur, and it is part of history. Incidents were few but well publicized and involved some local families. The inclusion of this part of the history of Davidson County is no different from other parts of the country and in no way detracts from the honor and achievement of those who did serve. Names of the deserters, however, have been left out of this section. JL)

By 1917, the European powers had been at war for three long years, and the American public followed the conflict with interest—and horror. Reports of long battles with hundreds of thousands of casualties in a single day were common in the local and national news. The publicity in the American press was one of the factors which made it difficult to recruit new members to the National Guard units and the regular army. All through the early part of the 1900s, appeals were extended to the various communities to add to the ranks of the troopers. Other reasons it was so difficult to persuade men to join were low pay, work schedules, family, and lack of interest to name a few.

The National Guard units had gone to Texas under strength, but in 1917 that was not an option. The deadly conflict that lay ahead made it imperative that the ranks be filled. Conscription was the only way this could be accomplished, and the law was duly passed on May 18, 1917. National Registration Day was set for June 5, after which lengthy lists of eligible men were published in local newspapers and notified to report to the local conscription board when called. Phones were not common, so the only way of contacting the men was through the press and the mail. Pay for the men was more than doubled to $65 per month for privates, other ranks accordingly.

The vast majority would go if called but in contrast to the willingness of most of the men, a few young fellows in the county had no desire to go fight for Uncle Sam. The news from overseas might have been too graphic or their ancestry may have been German, any number of reasons, including cowardice, caused these few to avoid induction or actually desert from the army. In either case they were listed as deserters.

Camp Greene, which had been established about the same time as Camp Sevier, was near Charlotte as a training camp for soldiers. It had also been designated as the lockup for anyone accused or convicted of desertion in North and South Carolina.

Penalties were severe for those who did not report or the few who actually deserted after induction. One year in jail and disenfranchisement was the minimum penalty although jail time could be much longer depending on the circumstances. The offending party would never be allowed to vote in an election or hold public office for life. There was no statute of limitations either. Some felt, having been told by friends or family, that all they had to do was hide out until the war ended and then everything would be all right. This was false information based on what some Southerners did in the Civil War, but there was no Confederate States of America at this time, and it was not 1865.

There were even accusations by federal authorities that local sheriffs were either failing to do their duty by arresting deserters or sympathizing with them. It seems that some local officers were reluctant to enforce federal law, arguing that only federal authorities could do so and it was not within their purview to do so. In May 1918, an article in *The Dispatch* stated that the opinion of the attorney general of North Carolina was that "all laws assume that the officials charged with the duties of serving criminal process will promptly discharge those duties." Mitchell County was judged the worst offender of this sort, with Davie County a close second.

Another way slackers thought they could avoid the draft was by marriage. Beginning just after the declaration of war, April 6, the marriage licensing bureau, established in 1913, saw a marked increase in applications. Some were misinformed grooms, and others were anxious brides who thought that marriage would exempt the boy from military service. They were wrong. Instead, the government caught on quickly and made it known that hurried marriages of that kind would move the draftee's number up the list. (All men eligible for the draft were assigned a number by the local draft authorities whether or not they were to be called.)

In the summer of 1918, a suit of soldier's clothing was found in the woods south of Thomasville. It was obvious that the wearer had deserted while on leave and changed to civilian clothing. Unfortunately for the deserter, he left a letter from his wife in the pocket with both of their names included. This deserter was from Mt. Olive, North Carolina, and was not a part of the local community. Why the clothing was found near the city is a mystery. He was probably quickly captured although no further report of the incident appeared in the news.

Deserters of the other kind, those who just refused to report for induction, were given every opportunity to mend their ways before being classified as criminals. The local conscription board sent a letter to the draft dodgers, notifying them that they were required by law to report. If they did not, a second letter was sent after one week, giving them ten days to come forth. Failure to appear then meant that their names were listed on the front page of the newspaper. A week after that a warrant was issued for their arrest usually accompanied by a $50 reward. Even then, if they would report before being captured, they would be sent on to one of the military camps. Not only that, but also if the offender reported late, he was deemed automatically fit for service. No medical examination was given and no exemptions were allowed at that point so that any exemptions the party might have had would not even be considered before induction.

As late as summer 1918, delinquents were given one last chance to report without consequence. Special Officer Fredrick C. Handy from Mitchell County apparently was a fair but stern officer. Notices were sent, by newspaper and letter, to all delinquents to report by June 28 at 9:00 a.m., and they would be inducted without prejudice. If needed, the government would even provide transportation to the meeting place whereupon the recruit would be accompanied to military camp to make sure the new soldier was not ridiculed or made to feel anything but welcome. Handy was working in Davie, Davidson, and Randolph Counties at the time. At the appointed time, ten men from Davidson and eight from Davie showed up and were escorted to Camp Greene, not to the brig, but for military training. No report was found for Randolph, but the results were probably similar to the other counties. That left about ten men in Davidson who were still in hiding.

Chief of Police Walker and a patrolman named Clodfelter assisted by Lieutenant Newton got word of a couple of deserters in the county who were members of the 119th Infantry and had been gone from Camp Sevier for about three weeks. When the police officers entered the home, the boys put up a little fuss, but the wife of one of them put up a real fight. Grabbing a knife from the table, she swung it at one officer, cutting him on the hand. She caught the other officer on the arm, but he was wearing a heavy coat and was unharmed. The deserters seemed to submit peacefully when the officers brought out the handcuffs, and all three were escorted to the local jail. Asked why they deserted, they answered that they had been down in the county running a still.

Up in Midway, prime farming country at the time, there was a family of deserters—two brothers and a first cousin. Deputy Marshalls H. C. Trott of Salisbury and G. M. Thompson of Davidson County formed a posse of the following men: Deputy Collector F. C. Talbert, Deputies David Graham and A. L. Nash from Salisbury; Government Inspector J. M. Newton of Thomasville; Deputy Sheriff L. Newsom from Winston-Salem; A. Hoke Harrison, C. F. Caudle, and Deputy Sheriff Fred Sink of Lexington. The community in which the deserters were living was smack in the center of all of the jurisdictions of the posse.

Investigations revealed that the three boys were said to have many powerful weapons about them and enough ammunition to hold off any intruders. Threats had also been made to neighbors and against anyone who would come to arrest them. The deputies were also aware that the father might also support the boys should a struggle ensue.

Early one morning the posse gathered in a hotel lobby in Winston-Salem to plan the arrest. The offenders were known to be at one of two places, and they had to decide which one. The decision being made, surprise was essential. Before daylight the posse rode to Midway to the house they had selected as most likely harboring the deserters. As the automobiles came to a halt, some of the deputies surrounded the house while three others broke into the home, arousing the occupants who began to scream. Rushing up the stairs, one of the deputies kicked in a bedroom door and discovered all three subjects hurriedly getting dressed. All submitted meekly to the arresting officers.

In the house it was found that the rumors of an arsenal were true. A brief search turned up three loaded double-barreled shotguns, four Colt pistols, a pair of brass knuckles, three high-powered rifles, and plenty of ammunition for all the weapons.

Taken before the exemption board that day, the boys claimed that they had acted entirely of their own accord and that no one had helped them in any way. The father of two of them had been arrested with them, so the boys were trying to protect him from prosecution, but in doing this the boys confessed to desertion. Bail for the father was $1000 and was paid by a county commissioner. The boys were immediately shipped off to Camp Greene for trial.

(The officers were not through for the day. Later on the posse went to the home of two known moonshiners which were called "bushwhackers" in that time, but the brothers had gotten wind of the earlier arrests and had fled. Their mother promised to try to persuade them to turn themselves in, the deputies promising that if they did not, the boys would be tracked down relentlessly.)

Two other Davidson County men, one from Thomasville, also refused to report for the draft; and one of them was mortally wounded by officers. He had been arrested for desertion and lodged in the local jail a few weeks earlier, but one of his friends sawed a hole big enough to escape and both of them took off. A couple of weeks later, an unnamed citizen got the drop on the two and was holding them for deputies when a friend of the deserters put a gun to the citizen's head and bade him to drop his weapon. Then all three hightailed it into the countryside. Next day, deputies located them all at their still near Gordontown—they were bushwhackers as well as deserters—and attempted to arrest the criminals. Shots were fired, and the three perpetrators were wounded, one mortally, while the other two escaped. They were later captured.

Near Denton, Special Officer Handy went to the home of a deserter whose number had been called. The officer told the father that he knew where the boy was hiding and would get him sooner or later, so it would be best if he were to give himself up voluntarily. A little while later the boy did appear, and he was inducted. However, when time came to report for duty, the boy disappeared again and was dodging officers. No further account was found as to whether he was captured or not.

Another local actually went to Camp Sevier, deserted, and was captured several weeks later at his father's house. He was taken directly to Camp Greene for incarceration instead of the local jail, it being unnecessary to have a civilian hearing.

Probably the most frightening incident of all in the county did not really involve bushwhackers or deserters. Federal authorities were quick to notice that seven high-powered rifles had been purchased and sent to one location near High Rock. Although the feds investigated the matter thoroughly—the owners claimed they were to be used for self-defense because of increased lawlessness in the county over the draft—a close eye was kept on them for months afterward.

On October 30, 1918, *The Dispatch*, Thomasville Department included the following item: "It is understood that nearly all the deserters in Davidson have been brought in and sent to the camps and jails where they are awaiting court-martial proceedings. Mr. Young carried four or five away last week that he had captured in this county and Randolph together."

CHAPTER EIGHT

CAMP SEVIER

~~~~

We sincerely trust that Hon. L. D. Robinson will join Congressman Doughton in his fight in Congress for taxing dogs as a means of raising war taxes. The Dispatch, *Thomasville Dept. August 8, 1917*

~~~~

When the National Guardsmen had been nationalized, the United States was not really ready to fight. Even the United States regular army was a token force, and the marines were considered part of the army. By the time the Thirtieth Division was fully organized, General Pershing had been made commander of all American troops and had landed in France on July 3, 1917, with a few divisions of regular soldiers, called "doughboys" and some marines, sometimes also called by that name, much to their displeasure. This was the first contingent of the American Expeditionary Forces (AEF) in Europe. However, lacking equipment, supplies and, most of all, training, it would be many months before the Americans were ready to fight.

The principal Allied combatants welcomed the Americans and began demanding that they be "amalgamated" into the French and British armies. Pershing was to have none of that, however. He insisted that the American troops fight under the American flag. The Brits and French were adamant, but so was Pershing (and Wilson). The stalemate meant that action by most of the Americans would be delayed until 1918, during which time they would receive training.

As the marines and the regulars trickled into France, the top commanders continued to wrangle with just how they were to be used. The British and French wanted them fed into the front lines immediately, but Pershing insisted on Americans fighting under American command only. British Commander General Sir Douglas Haig and overall commander French General Ferdinand Foch hounded Pershing constantly over the supposed lack of involvement by the American soldiers. It was even rumored that Foch was being urged to have Pershing replaced, although how the French commander could accomplish this feat was not explained. From the point of view of the French and British, the Americans were not being used properly, and this could cause the Allies to lose the war. (Some historians claim that it almost did just that. The debate still goes on today.)

A newspaper article after the Thirtieth Division was formed listed the men of Company L as follows, mistakenly using the old designation of Third Brigade.

Roster Co. L, 3rd NC Infty., Thomasville, NC, Aug. 30, 1917:

Captain	C. H. Newby		
1st Lieutenant	W. B. Stone		
2nd Lieutenant	R. O. Little		
1st Sergeant	D.C. Culbreth		
Supply Sergeant	R. B. Talbert		
Mess Sergeant	Paul Green		
Sergeants:	R. J. Westmoreland	J. M. White	L. D. Player
	C. W. Harrison	J. S. Burton	S. A. Myers
Corporals.	J. S. Stratton	D. B. Barkley	E. L. Wood,
	J. H. Burrus	L. C. Irvin,	H. F. Fraylick,
	W. F. McGee	W. S. Wilson	W. H. Hulin
	O. C. Herman.		
Cooks.	J. H. Fletcher	B. C. McSwain	
Mechanic	W. C. Fitzgerald.		
Buglers	F. B. Creakman	Paul Shoaf.	
Privates	G. W. Broadway	J. M. Briles	McLaurin Baker
	J. L. Barkley	D. W. Biggerstaff	G. G. Clinard
	B. Cornelius	C. C. Cook	J. B. Clemmons
	E. H. Davis	R. E. Davis	S. Daniels
	H. M. Flynn	W. C. Fouts	E. E. Freedle
	R. Gurdner	B. M. Hager	L. P. Hiatt
	H. D. Harris	I. H. Harris	N. M. Hopkins

P. M. Hall	W. S. Hall	Bob Ivey
Carl Jackson	J. A. Klass	E. H. Leonard
M. M. Leonard	Speight Laughlin	R. L Loftin
J. M. Lambeth	Jesse Mann	Walter Morgan
J. T. Murphy	G. W. Murphy	H. H. Murphy
G. M. Marks	R. C. McRae	R. P. Myers
R. P. Osborne	G. C. Pressley	S. A. Russell
Harvey Ramsey	Max Rothrock	W. L. Smith
Wiley Spencer	R. Y. Shaw	E. A. Stone
H. E. Sullivan	W. S. Sanders	B. M. Sanders
T. S. Saunders	G. E. Tesh	Willie Tomlinson
W. R. Westmoreland	J. D. Watson	C. M. Williams
L. H. Welborn	J. D. Winslow	M. A. Yarborough.

Stewart Westmoreland

Daniel C. Culbreth was promoted to second lieutenant during the fall of 1917.

Hammett D. Harris was the youngest of five children, was a tall young man, six feet one inch, but slender, weighing in at only 150 lbs., with red hair and penetrating grey eyes. His mother had died when he was but two years old, so he was raised by his father, Mr. T. F. Harris and his older sisters. In 1912 he left for Florida to work in the orange groves and even bought a small one for himself, but by 1914 he was back in Thomasville where he began to farm as a career. He enlisted in the local Company L upon his return and was a mason as well as an active member of Main Street M. E. Church. Like many of the other men, he was discharged from the National Guard in August 1917 and immediately reenlisted in the U.S. Army's Thirtieth Division.

Sam Myers was also tall and lanky with fair hair and grey eyes. He had served with Company L from 1913 until April 1916 when he was discharged. Next day he was reenlisted as a sergeant for the Blues. He was an expert with the rifle and consistently scored high in the shooting meets. A woodworker by trade, probably at one of the chair factories, he was only twenty-four years old in 1917. His brother, Paul, also joined Company L.

Haymore Westmoreland would not survive the war. Born in Stokes County, his family moved north of Thomasville to farm and raise a family. His mother died of measles when Haymore was just a child, and his father remarried soon after. The lad would accept his stepmother as truly his own and the bond between them was as strong as if she had been his real mother. A few months after his nineteenth birthday, answering the patriotic call of the community, he joined the hometown Blues on April 9, 1917, and went off to Camp Sevier with his new friends a few months later. Two days before leaving for South Carolina, his father bought him a new suit and took him to the photographer. His engagement to Mattie Sapp was put on hold by his enlistment.

Earnest and Curtis Gurdner were brothers from Johnson City, Tennessee, but "Ern," as he was called, took up residence in Thomasville sometime prior to 1916, probably for the same reason as so many others—a good job. He was on the roster of men who went to Camp Stewart with the Blues that year. In the patriotic fervor that swept most of the nation after the declaration of war, Curtis enlisted in Thomasville so that he could be with his brother. Both had black hair, but Earnest had a dark complexion while Curtis was fair. Ern was skinny but tall at six feet three inches and 150 lbs., just five pounds more than his little brother who stood only five feet ten inches.

Except for a few enlistees like these, recruitment was slow for the North Carolina battalions. Captain Newby could not understand why the hometown boys would not volunteer, preferring to wait to see if they were to be drafted or not. This was common throughout the nation that summer. Since not enough volunteers to from North Carolina were forthcoming, the ranks were opened up to men outside the three states. Draftees were sent to Camp Jackson, South Carolina, for their initial training sessions, then they might be transferred to Camp Sevier after a few weeks. As these conscripts arrived at Sevier, most were asked about their home during their first formation. Several answered "Davidson" and were later detailed to A or L. The same held true for other sections. Several Davidson boys were picked up by the home companies upon arrival at Sevier this way. Still, though, the ranks were not filled, so men from Indiana, Kentucky, Illinois, and the Dakotas were eventually welcomed into the formerly exclusive hometown units. It was still a Thomasville unit (and Lexington), but this marked the end of the old era of exclusivity of regiments.

~~~~

I would state that I personally interview[ed] Pvts. Noble P. Brown and William R. Stewart as to why they were transferred from Camp Jackson, Columbia, S. C. to Camp Sevier, Greenville, S. C., and they know of no reason whatsoever why they were so transferred—Captain 120th Inf. Comdg. Co. L

~~~~

Harrison Sullivan and Haymore Westmoreland at Camp Sevier in 1917.
[Photo courtesy of Yvonne Stewart]

Before long British and French instructors, fresh from the front, arrived to begin training the men. This was not just bayonet and target practice but classroom work as well. Officers were sent to special training, some in Texas, while sergeants and enlisted men learned tactics. Trench warfare was taught, of course, but being Americans, the soldiers were also trained in offensive strategy. The British had been trained to fight as a unit and to follow the original orders to the letter, come what may, but the Americans were told to think for themselves if need be. This radical idea would serve the doughboys well when they arrived at the front. By this time, the third year of the war for the British and French, lessons learned early in the war were now being passed on to their American students. The early practice of massive assaults by thousands of men had finally been discarded as too costly. Everyone, including hometown newspapers, thought they would be in France by Christmas 1917.

Classes were set up to train the men in the use of the French *chauchat* rifle. This was a light machine gun with a flexible bipod mount and a circular magazine, open on one side. It was widely used throughout the war by the French and later the Americans. It could be fired from a prone position and also while standing, walking, or hooked to the belt of the soldier, but it could jam easily due to the design of the magazine. R. O. Little had become an expert in the use of this weapon and was one of the instructors at Camp Sevier.

A major hitch in training occurred in the middle of December 1917. Winter, generally mild in South Carolina, took a turn for the worse. Snow fell for days, water froze, and the bad weather lasted for more than a month. Training was virtually at a standstill while the men cut firewood just to keep from freezing. Toward the end of January, milder weather finally arrived and training recommenced.

In his letters, Haymore Westmoreland always expressed his desire to go home for a visit. On one occasion when he was scheduled to do so, he fell and cut his eye, so the trip was canceled; on another occasion the trip was canceled by a two-week bout with the mumps; in still another, he seemed to have had a dreamlike experience:

Little Blossom

1. Oh dear! ise so tired and lonesome. i wonder why mama dont come. she told me to sut up my blue eyes and fore i waked she'd be home se said she was going to see T a m m a se lives by the

river so bright i spect my mama fell in ther and praps wont turn home tonight.

2. I diss im afraid to stay up here without any fire are light but dads [gods] lighted the lamps up in heaven i seen all twinkling and bright I think Ill go down and meet paper Is pose he has stoped at the store. it's a great pilty store full of bottles. I wish he would nt go there any more.

3. Some times he is sick when he comes and he stumbles and falls up the stairs and once when he come in the parlar he kicked it my poor little chair and mama was all pale and frightened and begged me up close to her breast and caled me her poor little blossom and gess ive forgotten the rest.

4. But I member that papa was angry his face ? was so red. and wild and I member he strucked at poor mama and hurted his poor little child, but I love him and diss Ill go find him praps he'll come home with me soon and den [?] it wont be dark and lonely wating for mama to come.

5. Out in the dark went the baby her little heart beating with fright till the [The letter ends here.]

Haymore was homesick throughout camp. His letters home typically expressed the fact that he did not like army life. In one such letter, he complained about having to work on Sunday, "You bet thay work son day as same as Monday hear you dont no when sunday come down hear and i dont like work to work no sunday you no i never like to work no sunday well we have to get up every morning at five a clock and it is work all [illegible] in the men that the way we have to work down hear how you like that I dont like it much."

On the other hand, Westmoreland made a lot of friends at camp; Harrison Sullivan was one, and Hammet Harris was another. It may have been that Haymore only wrote home when he was melancholy because some of his letters do give hints of having a really good time, "I drill ever ry day and have a big time every night." The reference to the night time activities alluded to the fact that the boys were free to do as they pleased at night, and Greenville was not off-limits.

By mid-February, the camp routine had become monotonous, but rumors of deployment to France soon began to surface. The word was expected any day to break camp and head north. Wives who had come to live in Greenville to be near their husbands were packed and ready to go home when the boys left. It was a nervous but exciting time for all concerned. Captain Leonard and Major

Phillips were in an advance party sent to France early to make preparation for the division there. Lieutenant Joe Cecil was left in command of Company A.

The winter weather finally gave way to warmer days and nights, and the regiment became restless. It was time to put to use all that they had learned for the past several months. Not only was camp life becoming monotonous, but also the urge to get to France and get the fighting over with was on the hearts and minds of all the men. Of course there was fear of the unknown, but that was secondary to getting on with the mission for which they had been trained.

Haymore Westmoreland on March 16, 1918, wrote to his stepmother, "Dear mother I aim having a haird time a long now but hope to find it better some time Dear dont study about me I will get a long some how I study a bout you every day and hope you dont study a bout me as much as I do Well Dear we planty to eat and we get planty of close to ware and we dont study a bout intiny to study a bout so we have a good time."

Then it happened. In April, post exchanges were ordered not to place any more orders and to let the inventory dwindle, a sure sign of movement. Finally in early May, camp activity hit high gear, and one or two regiments at a time began to move out. It had been almost a year since they had been absorbed into the regular army as the Thirtieth Division formed, and they had encamped at Camp Sevier. They had spent that time training for their mission while the logistics of deployment were worked out. They were ready.

> "We are to leav in a few days for finch it wont be but few deyes about teen days till we [?] go to frinch I thought I would get to come home bee for I had to go to frinch but thay sad thay would not give no more pas [?] I wont get to come home no more to see you all but hope to come back bee for long dont you all study about me I will write to you all wher I aim at we are we air get ready to leave to day but we will stay hear afew days bee for we go to frinch I hate to leave camp sevier it seems like home [?] we have sty hear so long till it seem like a home to us I have some frind at Greenville I told good by sonday we keant go to town no more I aim so tired tell keant wait good I have work all day hard I did not fild like writ to you night but I sad if I did no write to you to night I would have time in more we have got so much work to do that it take us all the tim to do it so I will close for this time hope to hear from you all real soon from your son Hay more west moreland"

Above: Rifle pits at Camp Sevier. General Pershing was furious when he was told the men were being trained in trench warfare. (NARA II) Below: The winter storm of 1917-1918 interrupted training for almost a month. L-R: Lt. Dan Culbreth, Captain C. H. Newby, and 1st Lt. R. O. Little. (Courtesy: Patsy Henderson)

Indeed it was a busy time. The whole camp was busy day and night as they packed up everything they would need, wrote last-minute letters, said good-bye to loved ones who had come to stay in Greenville, and a million other things in order to get ready to go.

Over a period of three days beginning May 7, 1918, the 120th was sent northward to Camp Merritt, New Jersey, for transport to England, then France. The train route was supposed to be top secret, but the route the boys were to take was no secret at all. Part of the group went via the Charlotte to Greensboro to Lynchburg route, and the others went via the Greenwood to Raleigh to Richmond route through North Carolina. Either route made it fairly easy for family members to at least be at one of the rest stops to bid their man a last farewell. The excitement was electric as the troop trains traveled through the Tar Heel state. All along the tracks, people turned out cheering and waving flags so that the passage was accompanied by a "continuous ovation" from the southern border all the way into Virginia.

In fact, the train did stop in Thomasville for about five minutes. Family and friends crowded the downtown area as the soldiers poured from the train for a few precious moments with their families. The men knew that this was the last time they would see their loved ones for some months or even years, and this last good-bye was emotional for them. Some, of course, would never see their loved ones again.

Haymore Westmoreland's father did go to the station to see his son. A few days later Haymore wrote, "Thay was a big crod thare i look for you but i did not see you i seen all my friend at home. good By for me [illegible] i will come back some time to see you all I hope dont study about me for a wile write to you all every time I can Good By for a long time hope to see you all a gan Good By for this time from Hay more westmoreland may god bless you all till i see you a gan xxxxxxxxxxxxxxxxxxxxxxxxxxxxxxxxxxx [kisses] look at this and thank off the one ho write this good Bye All."

CHAPTER NINE

DEPLOYMENT

The 120th may have reunited briefly at Camp Merritt, New Jersey, by nightfall on May 11, but First and Second Battalions, plus Supply Company, quickly departed by train the next day to Boston, Massachusetts, leaving the rest of the men behind. The day after that they departed Boston on the Bohemian—a dirty, unsanitary, and foul-smelling ship about which the men complained the moment they set foot on her decks.

As Camp Merritt was just north of New York City and drilling was impossible, the rest of the 120th were granted leave to do some sightseeing. Private Westmoreland wrote, "I went over to new york last night to see the city now you aut to see the city it is a big place there I stad there all day and I did not see the town I had a fine time."

Six days after the first units sailed, Third Battalion, Regimental Headquarters, Headquarters Company, and the Machine Gun Company departed from Boston on the HMAT Miltiades. After sailing back to New York to join their convoy, the Miltiades headed east toward Europe on May 20. It would be three weeks before they caught up with the rest of the regiment.

The second night out, the Miltiades was not able to keep up with the convoy and lost contact with the other ships about 6:00 p.m. Consequently, the ship diverted to Halifax, Nova Scotia, arriving there next morning to await another convoy. The ship may have had another purpose in going to Halifax because two men from the Machine Gun Company were taken ashore and admitted to the hospital. Twenty-four hours later, they set sail again for England in company with another slower flotilla. That was about all the excitement the men had on the trip over; in fact it was all rather boring once they got over the initial excitement of being on the open sea for the first time.[6]

The most excitement on the voyage seemed to have been caused by the food. The Bohemian was of British registry and the galley, therefore, prepared British-style food. The Southern boys were accustomed to biscuits, beef, and fried chicken, but there was none of that on board. Kidney pie, mutton, and orange marmalade were not to the liking of the Southerners. The marmalade was the worst, disgusting to the extreme to the Southern taste, so much of this delicacy was "heaved" overboard, some of it still in the containers, and most of the boys remembered the foul taste for the rest of their lives.

The Bohemian had also diverted to Halifax where the ship, characterized as a "tramp steamer" by the daily logs, was cleaned from bow to stern, but the first order of business was to get some more palatable food for the men who were suffering from "extreme hunger." American cooks took over the galley, causing an immediate spike in morale, and the men's usual good humor returned.

The differences between the two ships could not have been more pronounced. The Bohemian, earlier described, was a "skow" whereas the Militiades was apparently much more pleasant. No complaints about the food were recorded, and the ship by all appearances was neat and clean. Not only that, the commanding general of the Sixtieth Brigade, S. L. Faison, plus Major Sidney Minor, commander of the 120th Infantry were on board. Just as importantly, the band of the 120th was also taking the trip with the officers.

On the evening of May 28, 1918, the band gave a dinner concert for the officers of the Sixtieth Brigade. Appetizers of "boiled steinbass" with anchovy sauce, followed by calves' sweetbreads americaine and brinjal farcie. The main course consisted of braised ribs of beef printaniere, corned leg of lamb with parsnips, duck a la bigarade, accented with vegetable panache, and roast and boiled potatoes. Desserts were Bakewell Pudding, fruit tart, and pastries. Cheeses and coffee rounded out the meal which was followed by a musical "programme" by the band wherein marches by J. P. Sousa, the overture "Maritana," a cornet solo, and various selections by request were played.

---

[6] Daily reports for Headquarters, Machine Gun Company, and Third Battalion all mention the diversion; but each reason given is different from the others.

Above: The H.M.T. Miltiades of Australian registry which
transported half of the 120th regiment to Gravesend, UK.
(Courtesy North Carolina Department of Archives; Bynum M. Grogan Papers.

The Miltiades with Company L on board on their way to France.
Other ships in the convoy can be seen in the distance.
(Courtesy: Jay Harry Tesh)

Back in the real world, lookouts were always on the alert for German U-boats, and some were spotted, but no damage was done to the ships. Days passed easily enough, but the nights were quite a different story. On the open ocean late at night, the pitch blackness made it seem rather eerie to the inexperienced country boys, there being no reference points except for the stars. The only sounds were those of the quiet engines and a feeling of loneliness as the ship plied the calm waters. The world seemed very far away at night. As they neared England, they were joined by several subchasers which escorted the convoy the rest of the way to port.

The interim destination for the Bohemian was Liverpool, England, in the northwest, on May 27, and for the Miltiades, Gravesend, on the Thames opposite London on June 4 where they billeted for the night. Why the two transports carrying one regiment landed at different ports eight days apart is open to speculation, army wisdom being as good as any. After a "leisurely" voyage from Boston, the pace really picked up after landing in England for both sections. Each man was presented with a welcome card bearing the signature of "George RI," King George V, as the men walked down the gangplank then to waiting passenger trains. Sightseeing was limited to passing views from railroad cars and short stops to stretch cramped limbs. The stay in England was only as long as the hurried trip to transports at the English Channel.

Rather than waiting to be reunited with the rest of the 120th, the first group which included Company A immediately entrained for Dover then across the English Channel to Calais. Early on June 5, the boys left for Dover where they arrived about 3:30 p.m. and boarded transports immediately for the four-hour voyage to Calais. At this point, they were still several days behind the rest of the regiment.

(The account given in *The Thirtieth Division in the World War* was that the second unit landed at Gravesend, entrained for Dover, and crossed to Calais all in the same day—June 5. However, the logistics of this maneuver would have required the men to arrive in the early morning hours, leave almost immediately for Dover, then rapidly board transports for Calais probably arriving there late at night. It is certainly possible for this to have happened, but highly unlikely. In any event, the two sections of the 120th were both in France by June 5, 1918, though they were hardly within hailing distance of each other.)

This "forwarding camp" at Calais was the landing point for all British and Americans going to the front, and they were not to stay there very long, just a few days. As the men came down the gangplank, they could hear the noise of battle in the distance for the first time. The realization that they were in the fight now must have made quite an impression on the boys from small-town America. The men were marched to Camp Number 6, where they were billeted for refitting and orientation. The first sections of the 120th had already moved out of the orientation camps to await the arrival of the rest of the men.

At this point in the war, American production was not at a point that it could supply the doughboys with arms, ammunition, and war materiel. Such equipment as the Springfield rifles on which the Americans had trained were also not of the standard caliber as the British weapons, therefore all equipment except their clothing was exchanged for British equivalents. The men quickly adapted to the Lee-Enfield rifle, shorter magazine—not as well balanced, but useable. Other exchanges were the campaign hat which had been worn since the inception of the National Guard units for the British-style helmet and an overseas cap for use while not in the front line. The helmet was metal with a wide brim and did not cover much except the crown of the head. (This same helmet was used by the American armies at the beginning of WWII.) The cap was made of wool, which was folded flat and tucked inside the tunic when wearing the helmet. The canvas or leather leggings were given up for "puttees," long strips of cloth, the same material as the wool uniform, for wrapping the legs. The men liked these much better than the leggings. Overcoats and personal nonessential personal belongings were turned in for storage.

After receiving their new rifles, the men naturally needed to get used to them. Consequently, the boys marched several miles to target ranges and expended thousands of rounds, familiarizing themselves with the Enfields. Bayonet training filled some of the other hours. Company A was somewhere nearby but too far away for exchanging pleasantries.

Above: Forwarding Camp #6 at Calais, France. Below:
Thirtieth Division troops inspect the Lee-Enfield rifles that had just been issued.
(Both Courtesy: NARA II)

ID Book issued to R. O. Little (Courtesy: Patsy Henderson)

When the Germans declared the resumption of unrestricted submarine warfare on February 1, 1917, they knew they only had a short period of time to drive the Allies out of the war before the American weight could be used against them. Accordingly, in a series of offenses beginning in March 1918, the Axis had begun an all-out assault on the trenches from Ypres in the north to Belleau Wood near Paris. A series of salients were punched into the British and French lines by the Germans where, once again, their advance stalled. The Germans could not advance any further, but the Allies could not push them back. However, the Germans in most cases occupied the high ground so any movement by the Allies was immediately thwarted as a result. Both sides once again settled into the necessity of trench warfare, and no significant movement of either of their armies was the result.

The biggest threat imposed by one of these salients was forty-three miles east of Paris. Just as the 120th arrived at Calais, two U.S. Marine regiments and the Twenty-third U.S. Army Division were heavily engaged in a pivotal battle at Belleau Wood. What turned out to be the German's last push for Paris was stymied by the gallant marines there. With little information about the strength of the Axis army, poor reconnaissance, and inaccurate French maps, the marines fought desperately to gain control of a wooded area, the scope of which was unknown to them. The battle raged for almost the entire month of June, the Germans finally pulling back from the bloody ground on June 25. A grateful French government renamed Belleau Wood to "Bois de la Brigade de Marine," meaning "Wood of the Marine Brigade." Both regiments were also awarded the "Crois de Guerre," France's highest military honor. This battle was the first use of the Marine Corps in the World War as a fighting unit and ultimately saved the Corps from extinction.

(The Marine Corps is usually given sole credit for victory in this battle but the Twenty-third U.S. Army fought just as valiantly and lost many a good man also. However, the army press was severely restricted in reporting the battle whereas the marine press was not. Therefore, published accounts of the marines' part in the battle was reported immediately, but the army waited two full weeks before receiving permission to write an account. By then all of the credit had gone to the marines where it remains. The modern Marine Corps may owe its very existence to this delayed report by the army since Pershing and others had previously wanted to absorb the corps into the regular army.)

Three Davidson County men who were in units other than the Thirtieth Division were killed in action in June. Private Carl Link from Tyro was drafted and sent to Camp Jackson, South Carolina, for training in 1917. He died in battle on July 16. Henry Traynham of Abbott's Creek had moved to California in 1911 to pursue his career where he joined the National Army in 1917 and was in one of the first National Guard units to go overseas. He was killed in action on June 19. Private Travis Thompson of High Rock who was drafted in 1917 was killed, also that month. All of these men were presumably killed at Belleau Wood.

The Germans had been stopped in their tracks, and that is where they would remain. It became clear that prying them from prepared positions would be extremely difficult. Fresh troops were desperately needed, and the Americans were there to fill this bill. Being fresh, even naïve, this was the time when the American way of fighting would meet the practical test as was stressed from the beginning of their involvement. The British tradition was to fight as a unit without question and follow the battle plan to the letter, resulting in massive casualties, but the doughboys were trained to think as squads or individuals, reacting and regrouping as the situations warranted. This battle plan was in contrast to the costly lessons of the early years of the war.

When the American Second Corps, of which the Thirtieth Division was part, arrived in France it consisted of six divisions, later expanded to ten. In order these were the Fourth, Twenty-seventh, Twenty-eighth, Thirtieth, Thirty-third, Thirty-fifth, Seventy-seventh, Seventy-eighth, Eightieth, and Eighty-second. In June 1918, five of these divisions were pulled out and assigned to other fronts, and in August three more were reassigned under American command, leaving only the Twenty-seventh (New York) and the Thirtieth to make up the Second Corps. Not only were eight divisions pulled out, but also the 113th Artillery Battalion was immediately reassigned for duty with other divisions. The 113th was never in battle with the Thirtieth Division. All these changes left the two divisions alone to make up the Second Corps.

In addition to all that, the corps had no commander at this time. Instead, Lt. Col. George S. Simonds, chief of staff, answered directly to General Pershing. It must have seemed to the soldiers that this unit had been shelved. Simonds was faced with the difficult task of outfitting and supplying the corps, which actually was not a full corps at all. Training for the orphans also was problematic, finally finding a solution in that the Americans would train and bivouac with the British. Accordingly, the first assignment was with the British Expeditionary Forces (BEF) at the Eperlecques Training Area under the overall direction, not command, of the British. However—and this was probably Simonds's greatest tactical triumph—the Americans would retain their American commanders and noncoms. The British were reluctant to this arrangement, but Simonds's perseverance ensured that his plan eventually prevailed. Overall tactical command of the Second Corps remained with the British, but no officers of the corps were replaced with Brits.

All this having been worked out, three days after arrival at Calais, the Third Battalion moved out for Nielles, part of the Eperleques Training Camp. At this point they were several days behind Company A which was with First Battalion at Uterque. Second Battalion bivouacked at La Montaire and Headquarters at Grasse Fayelle. For the duration the three brigades would move from one camp to another, near enough for consolidation, but always several miles apart. Company A, First Battalion was usually bivouacked with HQ, naturally, but the Thomasville boys were several miles away with Third Battalion. Once though, the Asheboro Company was a close neighbor of the Lexington unit. Billets were barns or old houses, and a bit of straw served as a bed.

The time spent with the Brits was not at all bad. In fact, the Southern boys got on very well with their British counterparts. Even though both sides spoke English, the Southerners at first had a hard time understanding the "Tommies" as they came to be called. There is no report of the opposite being true. There were many comical moments as the boys with the Southern drawl tried to understand their English counterparts and their "cockney" accents.

Soon, with the language barrier broken, training began in earnest. The Thirtieth must have been the best-trained army in history since, from the summer of 1917 through May 1918, they had been in constant training. Counting the maneuvers and sham battles in El Paso, they had been in one training phase or another for almost two years. Now, having arrived at the front, they were to spend at least another month undergoing more training under the British. The advantages were obvious: the British had been at this business for four long years; the mistakes made early in the war would not be repeated by the Americans; and being assigned to the British, the problems of supply for the orphan divisions had been worked out. The British food was still a problem for the Southern boys, but the chief of staff worked with the supply depot, instructing them in what kind of food to order for the Americans, and did what he could to make sure the two divisions were properly supplied.

The period from June 5 to June 28 was similar to basic training camp back in the States, except for the necessity to cram as much into one day as possible. Physical training, bayonet practice, target shooting, close-order drill, gas attack simulation, and many other basic training activities gave the men little time to get bored. Officers and senior noncoms attended classes on many other subjects, while the rest of the men drilled.

On June 28, the division entered into the plan devised by the British whereby the Americans would train in a rear area for trench duty, then pull back, so as to give them ample time to adjust and to rest. This meant that some officers with their squads spent a few days at a time at the front until it was time for them to take over entirely. For example, on July 12, Major Phillips; Captains Young, Page, Phillips, and Newby; four lieutenants, and four NCOs went forward in a reconnoitering party to the

Sgt. Clyde Tesh,
Gas NCO for Company L.
Courtesy: Jay Harry Tesh

front line trenches while the rest of the men carried out regular training in the rear. Then, for two or three days at a time the officers and doughboys stayed in the trenches before rotating to the rear as another squad took over. This part of the training was called "Phase A."

During this phase also, while in the rear, the men learned about the German weapons including the *meinenwerfers* and various types of poison gas. The former was a trench mortar mounted on wheels which lobbed shells or canisters high into the air to impact directly on the Allied trenches. A low muzzle velocity resulted in the shell or canister, tumbling in the air, causing a characteristic "shoop, shoop, shoop" sound which became very familiar very quickly. Despite the warning provided by the sound of the oncoming munitions, many Allied troops were killed or maimed by these weapons.

Every company had a Gas NCO who inspected and issued gas masks to the men. Responsible for the job for Company L was Sergeant Clyde Tesh, a Thomasville boy. Just twenty-two years old, a product of the northern part of the county, Tesh was only about five feet seven inches, but he took his duties very seriously and kept accurate notes regarding the training and the condition of gas masks for the men. After all, he was responsible for making sure the men in his company had the best chance to survive a gas attack.

It was not easy for the Gas NCOs to get their job done given that they were required by special order to hold classes and instruction for all the men in their company while the officers had other things to do with the men. A complaint by some of these NCOs generated a scathing order from headquarters to company commanders that the education of the men in gas warfare was as important as instruction on the rifle and bayonet and must be carried out.

The Germans used poison gas first, but both sides adopted its use, and it had been developed to be more and more lethal as the war progressed. Carefully timed to be released with prevailing winds, the gas still had to be used with extreme caution since wind shifts could and did blow it back over the men who released it. Railroad tank cars or tanker trucks were brought in and placed as close to the front as possible, then as the prevailing wind was deemed acceptable, it was released. The fog thus created would drift silently toward the enemy. Moonless nights were optimal for these attacks since the gas could otherwise be seen from far off, giving the intended victims plenty of time to put on their gas masks. By this late in the war, horses and pack animals were most affected by the gas, but even they had specially designed gas masks.

That is not to say that men were not injured or killed by gas. The development of gas artillery shells made delivery of the gas much more dangerous to the enemy since winds need not be taken into account. Phosgene gas and mustard gas were the primary types being delivered this way by the Germans. The latter incarnation was gelatin in form and stayed that way below room temperature. Many Allied soldiers were unknowingly stricken by the gelatinous state of this gas during an attack. The yellow mass stuck to their clothing and as the temperature rose, as in when the soldier returned to his quarters, the solid turned immediately to gas, affecting not only him but also his companions. It penetrated the clothing too, causing painful sores and blisters. It could also cause temporary blindness.

Front line duty was difficult in the extreme. It seemed that the British and French never learned how to cope with the trenches regarding hygiene and the basic necessities. Whereas the German trenches were built as though they were to remain for some time, that lesson was lost on the Allies. Many pictures of men worn down by just trench life give a grim shot of how these enlisted men were forced to live. Hungry some of the time and dirty all the time, these men lived in the worst of conditions daily. The Germans even had electricity and underground bunkers, the British and French had dugouts and were exposed to the elements for days at a time. Their feet would sink in mud ankle-deep when it rained, and they would choke on dust when it was dry. Toilets were only slit trenches or dugouts in the walls of the bunkers. The stench was horrible. Tiny insects called "cooties" (lice) ravaged the bodies of the men while in the trenches. There was no getting rid of the pests, so the men just had to put up with them as best they could. Letters home from all the boys give a vivid description of the tiny insects which plagued them daily.

In the rear camps, water for showers had to be transported as far as ten miles, and then the men were only allowed a few seconds under running water. Many a doughboy had himself all lathered up with no more water to rinse himself off. Wade Phillips wrote of learning to take three baths with just a pint of water.

The rotation of troops in and out of the trenches worked well enough, but the trenches themselves were no better than before. The men could at least rotate to the rear after their stint was over, then rest and rid themselves of the cooties, before being rotated back again.

The Second Corps once again had a commander when on June 15, Major General George W. Read, a member of "Pershing's Traveling Circus" (this was not a derogatory term) assumed that post. Major General E. M. Lewis became the commander of the Thirtieth Division, Brigadier General Samson Faison was commander of the Sixtieth Brigade, Colonel Sidney Minor over the 120th Regiment, and Colonel Wade Phillips commanded the Third Battalion. Phillips was close friends with both Captains Leonard and Newby and continued to write letters to *The Dispatch* about the adventures of the Davidson boys.

General Sir Douglas Haig, overall commander of the British Expeditionary Force, inspected the division in mid-June to congratulate them on their fine achievements in training. The Thirtieth was one of the divisions he requested to remain with the British Army. On June 30, Pershing himself inspected the troops.

All of the other American divisions were, at one time or another, visited by American entertainers. Famous singers, comedians, dancers, and others toured the area, bringing a little bit of home to the boys. That was not the case with the Second Corps. Being entrenched with the British, all of the entertainers bypassed the corps except for Elsie Janis, a vaudeville star. On July 23, the "Sweetheart of the AEF" entertained the boys very close to the front line. She alone seemed to realize they were there.

The second period of training or "Phase B" was begun on June 27. Movement closer to the front was required, so on July 2 with heavy packs and under a hot sun, the division moved out toward Belgium. On July 4, they crossed into Belgium, the first American soldiers, under arms, to ever set foot on Belgian soil. The Belgians were well aware of the date being Independence Day for the Americans so whole villages turned out waving American flags as the boys marched toward the front. That evening the division was bivouacked in the Poperinge Area at a place dubbed "Road Camp." Just four miles distant was the front, and the boys were in range of German artillery for the first time.

A very curious event took place on July 18. Bennett Williams, a Mocksville boy, arrived to take his place in Company L. Williams had been gone from the company since February 12, while the 120th was still at Camp Sevier, three months before the regiment sailed for France. How he obtained passage or why he was not jailed is a mystery, but charges for being absent would have to wait until after the war. Meanwhile, he would fight alongside his buddies.

Above: Lewis Gun team practices in mid-July 1918. This water-cooled light machine gun was easily moved and was used extensively in the fighting. The Lewis gun, famous for being a British weapon, was actually invented in 1911 by an American, Isaac Newton Lewis. Notice the hobnail shoes and canvas leggings of one doughboy and puttees on the other. Below: Another doughboy in practice. (Both Courtesy NARA II.)

The Thirtieth Division marches through St. Martin au Laert July 29, 1918.
The official caption for these photos stated that the town is in Belgium but it is in
France near the border between the two. The Thirtieth Division entered
Belgium on July 4. (Courtesy: NARA II)

Maybe Williams was accepted into the regiment because it needed every man it could get. From the time it landed on June 5, until after its last battle, the Thirtieth Division was never reinforced. The losses sustained in the coming battles would have to be borne by the command. Because of casualties, transfers of officers, and noncoms within the ranks were plentiful, but it would be near the end of the war before the thinning ranks were augmented by fresh troops.

CHAPTER TEN

YPRES

~~~~

Ben is dead. The Germans got him.

~~~~

The entry of the Americans into Belgium had an immediate effect on the British who were suffering from very low morale. It must be remembered that the Tommies had been in the trenches for almost four years. The men now on the front lines were worn down by the dim prospects of the war ever ending. The Americans brought with them a sense of optimism and hope that had been lacking in the British ranks for some time. When these smiling, laughing Yanks went marching through to the front lines, the mood among the Tommies instantly improved.

The Germans too had been suffering from low morale. Kaiser Bill, as he was called by the Americans, could have prevented the war but chose not to do so. Since 1914, his absolute rule over Germany had eroded to the point that he had little power of any kind because of the war, limited mostly to awards and ceremonies. His generals and field marshals, namely Ludendorf and Hingenburg, were then in control of all aspects of the war. Their opinion, kept secret from the troops, was that Germany could not win. However, in mid-June, just as the Americans were arriving in large numbers, Russia dropped completely out of the war due to the Bolshevik revolution. Free from a threat to their eastern front, Germany was able to shift several divisions of soldiers to the west to face the other Allies, and the carnage would go on. On July 30, 1918, Carlton Newby was promoted to major.

The destination of the Americans was the canal sector south of Ypres (e-per), pronounced "Wipers" by the English. This area had been fought over since 1914, being directly in the path of the Germans on their march to Paris according to the Schlieffen Plan. (In fact, if the Germans had stuck to the Schlieffen Plan, they would have taken Paris and the war would have ended in 1915. The pivot point where, flushed with victory, they had celebrated too soon was at Ypres.) They had been stopped here, and several major battles had raged for its possession. The British Thirty-third and Forty-ninth Divisions were on "guard duty" here, expecting another major offensive by the Germans at any time. Far from being a quiet front, artillery, mostly British but some German, was continuous. Sporadic fighting took place almost every day and night, but major advances by either side were impossible.

Rotation into the front lines in Phase B exposed the men to this sporadic fighting, which produced the first casualty from Company L. Private Hammett "Bud" Harris, a young man from Thomasville, well liked by all his comrades, and an inspiration to them as shown by his Christian manner, was killed by a German mortar shell about daylight on August 4, 1918. According to a letter to Harris's father from Lieutenant Little, Harris had not been feeling well for several days, so Captain Newby ordered Sergeant Stratton to assign him to guard duty in the rear area. Harris refused the assignment, saying that he would go forward with his comrades and "do his bit." While in the forward trenches, a German trench mortar round exploded, knocking off his helmet. While retrieving it, another round exploded nearby, killing him instantly. "He gave his life for one of the noblest causes the world has ever known . . . was not afraid and was always ready to do his duty . . ." Harrison Sullivan, a good friend, also wrote to his own parents, "Tell them to never worry as their son lost his life for a good cause."

The death of Hammett Harris was a severe blow to the morale of the Thomasville boys. The men of Company L all held Harris in the highest esteem, but his death also strengthened their resolve that the Germans would not win this war, at least if the Blues had anything to say about it.

On the morning of August 6, the king of England inspected the troops near the front lines. Along with British companies, the men were ordered to dress in their cleanest uniforms, leave their weapons behind, and get ready for inspection. The only ones to participate from the 120th were from Company A, probably because they happened to be in the rear and were able to clean themselves up. Soon, a touring car bearing the king, General Lewis, and several illustrious American officers drove up. King George V gave a quick salute, said a few words about the noble cause, then was quickly gone.[7] In the afternoon the king visited a trench system the men were constructing and walked about one hundred yards in it, asking questions to the men as he passed. He seemed very interested in their work.

The American Sixtieth Brigade finally relieved the British, including some kilted Highlanders in the front-line trenches of the Ypres-Lys Canal sector on August 15/16. The First Battalion deployed on the right, Second Battalion to the left, and the Third Battalion in reserve. Essentially the brigade was in a wait-and-watch mode characterized as "guard duty." This did not mean that there was any lack of localized fighting, however. Nightfall meant patrols from both sides were groping in the dark, looking for prisoners and probing the enemy's defenses.

It was also a sector that, according to Colonel Pratt, the division did not want. Mt. Kimmel, the only mountain in Belgium, loomed ahead, so close that the men felt the Germans breathing down their necks, observing every move, and dropping artillery rounds in their midst. "This is the worst bit of front in the whole line from Switzerland to the sea, and it is this sector that has been handed over to the Thirtieth Division. We can take care of it and will take care of it, but we do not want it and are willing that the British should keep their own 'white elephant.'"[8]

The 120th took their first prisoner of war here, a Chinese man. The Chinese were very valuable in the war as workers for the armies, and evidently this one had strayed too far afield. The questioning of this man created a humorous situation, which seemed incongruous to the danger of the front lines. His only answers to the repeated questioning were "yes" or "Calais," the only English words he knew. He was sent back by Captain Boddie, with the note "Here is a Chinaman captured near Post No. 5. He is either on leave or AWOL. In either case he picked a damn bad place to spend it."

For the Americans the offensive at Ypres, called the "canal sector," officially began on August 17, 1918, with the Sixtieth Brigade occupying the trenches formerly held by the British, the Fifty-ninth in reserve. Since Newby had departed for the United States on August 10, he was replaced by Wallace

---

[7]   This was all captured on newsreel and is available to researchers at National Archives and Research Administration II, in College Park, Maryland..

[8]   Diary of Colonel Joseph Hyde Pratt.

Stone who had been promoted to captain. First Lieutenant Little was second in command.

In order to help clear the way for the doughboys, on the night of August 26/27, parts of the Company L's Third Battalion were involved in springing a gas attack on the Germans. Gas was released only when the prevailing winds would carry it to the enemy. Being heavier than air, the cloud would creep across no man's land and into the enemy trenches as they slept.

On this night several railroad tank cars were pushed to the area across from the German trenches, but the wind was practically calm, so they waited. About 2:30 a.m. the breeze was judged strong enough, four miles per hour, to be effective and the gas was released. Unfortunately, some of the gas whipped around to the last cars and several of the men were overcome. Although gas masks were in place, the heavy cloud displaced the breathable air and at least four men died as a result, despite heroic action by a Sergeant Hinson who was in charge of the detail. Four times he reentered the gas cloud and carried men to safety. Two other men were never found despite searches carried out the next two days. None of the casualties were from Company L.

There were signs that the Germans were pulling back in this salient, so heavy patrols were sent out every night in order to capture prisoners and gain intelligence. These patrols were mostly unsuccessful in bringing back Germans, but one who was captured did state that Kemmel Hill, overlooking the entire area, was being evacuated by the Germans and was only lightly defended. Therefore, a planned relief of the Sixtieth by the Fifty-ninth was canceled because of the opportunity to advance in the wake of the German's pullback.

Early in afternoon of August 31, two platoons of about ten men each from the Third Battalion were ordered forward from different directions toward Middlesex Road, about one thousand yards from their own trenches. Second Lieutenant Dan Culbreth led one of the patrols, the purpose being to scout the forward lines and establish an outpost if possible. Before starting out Culbreth told his men that they were on a dangerous mission, to keep their courage up and have faith in God. Cautiously, the patrol made their way right up to the German dugouts and were able to get within a few feet without being detected. Stepping up to an opening, Culbreth fired twice with his .45 automatic killing two of the enemy. Fourteen more surrendered but as the patrol started back toward their own lines, an enemy sniper found Culbreth. Reportedly his dying words were, "My poor mother."

On their retreat to their own lines, the American patrol was decimated by small arms and machine gun fire resulting in several more men being killed and others wounded in the ensuing scramble back to friendly lines. It was a disaster, but the mission was accomplished—that being to determine if the enemy was there in force. This military maneuver showed just how green the American forces were in

Lieutenant Daniel C. Culbreth.

their first action against the enemy, but their daring and bravery were also on display.

Culbreth, one of the most popular members of Company L, was killed about 2:30 p.m. He was a daredevil according to some, and his death was not unexpected by most, including Captain Newby, who was back in the United States by the time word arrived at home about his death. Culbreth's death-defying deeds had regularly amazed his comrades in arms, and so upon his death, the prediction by Newby that he would not last thirty days had come true. Lieutenant Culbreth was an original member of Company L and had risen through the ranks from private to second lieutenant.

Daredevil maybe, but foolhardy, no. It is questionable as to why he and his men were sent forward in broad daylight with no help expected from his comrades. After all, he had been through the training for over a year, almost two if one counts El Paso, and probably would not have taken such a chance. The regimental orders were explicit, however, and the patrols were organized and sent forward. Once again, the deaths filled the rest of Company L with a new resolve to beat the Bosche and push them back into Germany.

About an hour after the death of Culbreth, at battalion headquarters, Haymore Westmoreland was on duty as a runner. His slight build—five feet six inches, 125 lbs.—and strong legs made him perfect for this role. As his name was called by the battalion commander, Major Boddie, he was ordered to take a message to the lieutenant in charge of Company L. Since Culbreth was dead, the note was probably intended for Lieutenant Little, but we do not know for sure.

> Pvt. Westmoreland was instantly killed by a sniper's bullet which hit him in the stomach. He had just started to carry back a message to the lieutenant—he was within ten feet of me when hit. We were in the open fields about two thousand yards to the right of Ypres on outpost duty; we had been on outpost duty for two days, holding the line. It was August 31. I am sure of the date as I had been wounded only a few minutes earlier. Bennett Cornelius was the next to volunteer to carry the message and was shot and killed by the same sniper. The message finally went through.
>
> —Testimony of Cpl. Herbart N. Flynn of company L, hometown Winston-Salem, North Carolina.

This report stated that Haymore died instantly but another that he lived for almost an hour after being wounded. As his life slipped away, his last thoughts must have been of home. The bodies of both Westmoreland and Cornelius were taken to the rear for temporary burial.

In all, the action on August 31, utilizing men from Companies L, K, M, and I, resulted in the deaths of one officer and fourteen enlisted men. One of the boys killed while with Lieutenant Culbreth was Curtis Gurdner, the boy who had come from Johnson City to fight alongside his brother. A sniper's bullet wounded Gurdner in the stomach, and he died before reaching the dressing station. Five others were missing in action, and seventeen were wounded. One of the wounded, Private Robert Hensley, died of his wounds in hospital on September 2.

The next day the First and Third Battalions advanced on and captured Moated Orange, Voormezeele, Lock No. 8, and Lankhof Farm, all key points in the Ypres salient, and consolidated their lines to the Twenty-seventh Division on the right flank. Former German strong points, located on or near the local canal, situated southeast of the town were in American hands. All points were taken by 7:30 a.m. against sporadic German resistance. On their left, the First and Third battalions of the 119th Infantry had assaulted and held key positions around Voormezeele a few hours before. The area taken covered about one square mile.

The war department was not the only source by which relatives learned of the death of a loved one. Notified by Uncle Sam that their son was missing in action, the parents of Bennett Cornelius anxiously awaited further word. When it came, it was not from Washington but from a friend in Company L, Corporal Arville Yarborough, who wrote, "Ben is dead. The Germans got him."

This battle which was fought for around the base of Kemmel Hill, the highest point in Belgium, in the afternoon hours of August 31 and the morning of September 1, claimed the lives of the following from Company L in addition to Lieutenant Culbreth, Cornelius, Gurdner, and Westmoreland:

- Pfc. Reuben E. Davis; Thomasville, 2:30 p.m.; killed by rifle fire while advancing on the enemy;
- Pvt. William C. Lowery, 4:00 p.m., killed by rifle fire;
- Pfc. John I. Smith, Hickory, North Carolina, 4:00 p.m.; killed by rifle fire while advancing on enemy trenches;
- Pvt. Leslie C. Fewell, Mississippi, 5:00 p.m.; killed by shell fire while on duty in front-line trenches.

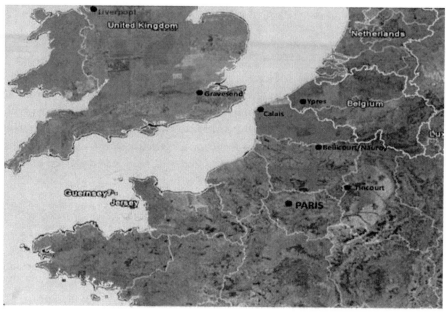

Above: Significant locations of the 30th Division in the war. Below:
Part of the Ypres-Commines Canal near Loch #8 after
30th Division secured the area. Courtesy: NARA II

In the afternoon of September 1, orders went forward to consolidate the lines and to expect shelling and a counterattack. On September 2, the 120th repulsed a strong counterattack by the German army which claimed Pvt. Nealie W. Watts, hometown unknown about 3:00 p.m., killed by shell fire in front-line trenches. The Americans, new to battle, had already learned to hold on to ground gained. Two days later, the Americans were relieved by the British and reassigned to the British First Army.

This small offensive and subsequent defensive action were the first major engagements for the men of the Thirtieth Division, and they performed well. The overall commanders took note of their eagerness to fight, so it was decided to pull the Second Corps out of that sector and move them to another portion of the front where heavier fighting was taking place. Despite their losses, spirits were high, and the men were ready to get on with the fighting.

The trip back on boxcars to the rest area was very uncomfortable, according to the reports of headquarters, and when they arrived they reported the billets as most unsanitary. Some time was spent in cleaning up, therefore, before the men could rest. But at the St. Pol area of France where they stopped for rest and refitting the distant sounds of battle faded entirely. The men were even able to take showers and get cleaned up, a luxury considering their actions of the past two months. They were also able to rid themselves of the incessant and irritating "cooties" for a while. The individual company camps were several miles apart, but during this time the men were able to see their friends and relations in Company A and others in K. Paris was only a few miles down the road, but the men were not allowed to go to the City of Lights much to the disappointment of many.

They could also see the devastation caused by the war. Major Phillips wrote about one village in a letter home, "There is a town right near which shows what war can do. Not a house left standing. Just great piles of brick and stone to show what used to be."

Having received their orders, Captain Newby and Lieutenant Dan MacRae had been sent home to train recruits and were not at the battle at Ypres. MacRae had been an original member of Company L, but was transferred to the Machine Gun Company when the Thirtieth was formed. Before assuming their new training duties, the two men paid a visit to Thomasville where they received a hero's welcome. An overflow crowd at the school auditorium listened to thrilling accounts of these officers' tales from the front. "Nobody in the world can fight like an American," exclaimed MacRae, and, "There was not a man in the Thirtieth Division that was more highly esteemed than Captain Newby in charge of Co. L."

Back in France, before being reassigned to headquarters, Major Phillips had been assigned to training soldiers for trench duty, and Captain Boddie had taken command of the Third Battalion. A few new men had been transferred to the company by this time from places other than Thomasville or North Carolina. The heart of the unit still called Thomasville home, however.

The American Second Corps was transferred to the British First Army on September 5, then to the British Third Army on September 17, and four days later to the British Fourth Army encamped on the Somme River. Now, thoroughly entrenched in the British Expeditionary Forces, the fellows must have felt quite distant from the rest of the Americans, but they did not have time to think about it. No one in the ranks resented the British, with whom they got along very well. General Read, for his part, seemed content to allow the British to take tactical control of the Second Corps, but the Americans never were under direct command of the British.

It was here that the Americans had their first encounter with the Australians whom they liked very much. The Fourth Australian Division was commanded by General Sir Henry Rawlinson and was one of the top fighting units of the entire war. After the war it was generally agreed that the Australians were the best fighters of any of the allied forces. The tactics practiced by the Aussies were better suited to the type of warfare prevalent in the Great War. Also, their bravery without foolhardiness proved to be exactly the right formula in war.

Because of the independent spirit exhibited by the Americans and Australians, the men of the two countries liked each other very much. The Americans liked the British too but not as well as the Australians. The camaraderie between the two "colonies" inspired the men to want to fight alongside one another.[9] Before long the Americans had begun to call the Brits "Tommies" and the Australians "Diggers," the latter a flattering term having to do with the work ethic of the soldiers from Down Under. In return, in addition to "doughboys"

---

[9]   The British still good-naturedly thought of the Americans as colonists.

the Americans were called "dogfaces" because they wore dog tags, slept in pup tents, fought in foxholes, and any number of other explanations for the name.

~~~~~

Eighty American divisions of 45,000 men each General March, chief of staff, told the house military committee today "should be able to bring the war to a successful conclusion in 1919." That is the number the army department plans to have in France by June 30, next.—The Salisbury Evening Post, *August 19, 1918.*[10]

---

[10] Major General Peyton March had commanded the First Field Artillery Brigade of the First Army Division in France. In March 1918, he was called to Washington to become army chief of staff. After the war, he successfully worked to abolish differences between the regular army, the army reserves, and the National Guard during wartime.

CHAPTER ELEVEN

THE THIRTIETH DIVISION'S FINEST HOUR

~~~~

Nothing between heaven and hell can stop a company of Tar Heel boys when the order is given to advance.—Letter from Milton Birkhead, Company K, January 18, 1919.

~~~~

The new sector where the Second Corps was to be sent was indeed hot. The Germans, though on the defensive, were still powerfully entrenched from the English Channel to Switzerland. Nowhere were they more confident of holding the Allies than at the Hindenburg Line. On September 22 the two divisions moved up to the Tincourt area and the following night, the 118th Regiment, Fifty-ninth Brigade relieved an Australian Division in the trenches, directly across the St. Quentin Canal from a place called Bellicourt, ninety-seven miles north-northeast of Paris.

Field Marshal Ferdinand Foch, the commander of all forces in Europe, had been persuaded to try an all-out push on four fronts against the Germans. The American army west of the Meuse River would attack toward Mezieres; the French, west of the Argonne River, would advance in the same direction and alongside the Americans; in the center the British Fourth Army would attack toward Bellicourt across the St. Quentin Canal; and the Belgians across Flanders toward Ghent. The main thrust of all the assaults would be the British center, to which the American Second Corps had been assigned. The Twenty-seventh and Thirtieth Divisions were assigned to that place of honor, and the 120th Regiment would spearhead the assault. The overall battle would be called the Somme Offensive. The Davidson County boys would be in for the fight of their lives.

By a series of maneuvers over the night of September 24/25, the 118th pressed forward to be in position for the assault, relieving the Australians, who retired to the rear. The 118th was entirely successful in this action but suffered many casualties. On the following day, the Germans attacked the Americans vigorously and were repulsed. This was the first major action in which the 118th was involved, and they performed admirably. The next day they were ordered to advance their line five hundred yards in order to improve the jump-off point for the main assault. Again the operation was successful.

Credit for some of their success must be given to the brave doughboys of the Twenty-seventh Division on the left. Over that same time period, the New Yorkers were scheduled to advance alongside the 118th but were unable to do so due to murderous flanking machine gun fire from Germans who held the high ground. Any advance made by these courageous men was severely contested by the enemy on their left flank and to their front. Therefore, the advances made by the equally courageous 118th would probably not have been successful without the efforts of the Twenty-seventh. The resulting line of the 118th was angled back to keep touch with the New York division. The consolidated lines were not as the command wanted them, but they would have to do. Even though it was extremely difficult to fall back or move forward for the Twenty-seventh, the assault was still set for the morning of September 29, but in order to catch up with the Thirtieth, they would push off one hour earlier.

From the beginning of these maneuvers, artillery rained down on the enemy incessantly. High-explosive shells as well as the new "BB" gas shells were used, the latter of which was similar to the German mustard gas. The bombardment had lasted for three days and used over a million rounds of various sizes of artillery.

On the night of September 27/28, in a steady rain, the 120th relieved the 118th for the main assault and encamped just west of Quarry Wood and Ravine. The relief maneuver was done under fire from the Germans resulting in two casualties to the Thomasville unit. As the regiment and others were filtering into the forward positions, at about 1:00 a.m., Pvt. Hubert Upchurch, Buena Vista, Virginia, and Pvt. William P. Smith, hometown unknown, members of Company L, were killed by artillery fire.

For the Americans of the 119th and 120th, their first brief glimpse of the terrain that awaited them must have chilled them to their core. The 120th was situated east and south of the village of Villaret; the 119th east of Hargicourt; and the 117th Regiment was in reserve to the west of those villages. The land was gently rolling, sloping down toward the St. Quentin Canal. The canal itself was banked by high cliffs where dugouts housed a large number of machine guns aimed directly at any assault from the other side and so well entrenched that any frontal assault was deemed impossible by both sides. A short distance to the east was a huge tunnel about a mile long, built by Napoleon, through which the canal passed. The Germans were able to house a full division of soldiers there in complete safety. Barges with the men on board could be moved in and out as needed. Artillery bombardment would have no effect on this tunnel.

Since the beginning of trench warfare, the Germans had been reinforcing the defenses at this point, believing it to be the most likely spot that the Allies would try to break through. Several times since 1915, British, Australian, and French forces had tried to do just that and failed each time, repulsed by the Germans. Confident in their defenses, the Germans never doubted that they could hold out there.

In front of and beyond the canal were several double rows of barbed wire of heavy iron forty yards deep in places and behind that were hundreds of machine guns and a staggering system of interconnected trenches, all wired for telegraph and telephone. This meant that the German defenders could quickly call for reinforcements wherever necessary. Huge concrete blocks studded with steel rods littered the landscape behind and among the barbed wire.

On the other side of the canal, the landscape sloped gently up toward Bellicourt to the north and onward toward Nauroy to the east. Thus situated, the terrain would provide almost no cover to the exposed doughboys. The advance, therefore, could only succeed by the grit and determination of the assaulting force.

According to Major William Graham, once of the Third Brigade, but then in the Second Battalion, the "Tar Heels were told before they went to the attack that they were going up against the hardest knot on the western front; that if they gained their objectives it would be possible to flank the German line on both ends and bring nearer the end of the war. In mild terms, they were told almost the impossible lay before them."

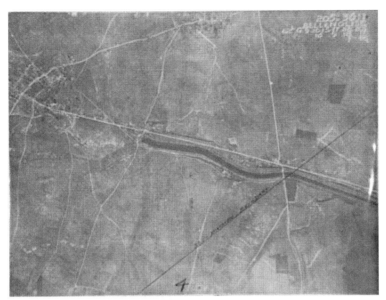

Aerial reconnaissance photos of the St. Quentin Canal (dark area in center above) and Bellicourt, left. The black line is the boundary for the Thirtieth Division's assault. Nauroy is at top center, Bellinglise at center where black line crosses the canal. Below: Detail of defenses around Bellicourt. Trenches and barriers front the city. Not visible are miles of heavy gauge barbed wire throughout the defensive system. Both photos taken September 24, 1918, five days before the attack. (Courtesy North Carolina Archives, Joseph Hyde Pratt Collection.)

Failure of this assault meant that the predictions by Winston Churchill and General Peyton March that the war would last at least to the summer of 1919 would be accurate, but there was no thought of failure in the minds of the North Carolinians.

There was, however, a sense of individual foreboding. Captain Ben Dixon, Company K, addressed his men for about an hour, made out his last will and testament, and wrote a letter for his mother back home. He said he did not expect to come out of this battle alive, but that his men should press on and take the objective even if there were only one man left standing. They loved him as a son loves a father, and the feeling was mutual. This stirring address to the men was remembered almost verbatim by the survivors of Company K for the rest of their lives.

All along the trenches on September 28, other men prepared for battle in their own way. Some officers made similar speeches to their men, some did not. Other letters home were written and last wills made and passed to the rear. Meanwhile, the men were equipped with 220 rounds of ammunition each, and two Mills No. 23 grenades. Hot food was brought forward, and each man was given enough rations for two days. Each regiment was also equipped with 600 No. 27 smoke bombs and 2,560 red flares, the former of which was to prove very useful.[11] Officers checked their men's equipment and rechecked them as the day dragged on.

Then it was dark. The rain had stopped earlier in the day, leaving the whole area slick with mud. Well, after nightfall on the twenty-eighth of September, doughboys from the American 105th Engineers began crawling out of the forward trenches in order to mark a straight path for the assaulting soldiers next morning. Keeping as low to the ground as possible, these brave men laid white tape parallel to and in front of the trenches, which exposed them to the Germans. Any noise they made quickly drew immediate machine gun fire from the enemy as well as gas canisters.

Lt. Col. Joseph Hyde Pratt of the 105th Engineers, Thirtieth Division, kept a detailed diary of all the action on his front during the war. Of this night he wrote:

---

[11] Maj. Gen. E. M. Lewis's account of the battle in the *Charlotte Observer*, April 6, 1919.

Today has been most exciting and tense. The day before the expected battle. [sic.] Many times I have read about the feelings of men as they waited for the dawn and the commencement of the battle, tonight I am going through that same sensation. The preliminary of the battle is now going on. The Artillery is firing on all sides, getting the range for their guns and testing them out in preparation of the awful barrage they are to put down on the enemy tomorrow morning. The tanks have gone forward to get into line for their part of the battle. The roads have been packed all day with lorries, wagons, automobiles, and troops all going forward to take their part in the coming battle.

Despite the harassing fire, the tape was well laid, later than intended, but in time for the assault to begin. Lieutenant Griffin, who led the engineers in the north sector, and several of his men were overcome by gas but his detail completed the task. Instead of returning to the trenches, the engineers, along with officers from the 119th and 120th, then lay in wait for the assault to begin. At 4:00 a.m. most of the doughboys began quietly crawling out of the trenches to positions along the white tape. By 4:30 a.m. on this Sunday, they were all in place. H Hour was set for 5:50 a.m. in order to give the men a chance to advance before sunrise.

The order of battle was as shown below:

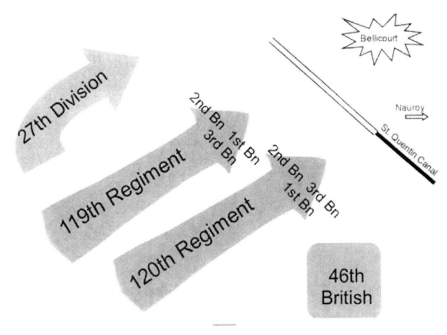

In the wee hours of the morning of September 29, the artillery that had been pounding the Germans went silent. The minutes and seconds moved slowly for the waiting Americans. One minute before the push off, the calm belied the coming battle, then, "As the final second came, the thunder of all ages seemed to break at once, the earth trembled and the flashes of hundreds of guns in the early dawn gave it all a fearsome aspect." [Col. Sidney Minor]

These were the American machine gunners opening up as the signal was given to go "over the top"; and the artillery which changed focus as it started laying down a protective curtain in front of the attackers as well as keeping the Germans pinned down in their positions. All along the line the doughboys began moving forward. The Third Regiment of the 120th was out in front, K (Asheboro) and M (Durham) Companies leading I (Burlington) and L (Thomasville). Those few still in the trenches joined their comrades who were already forward and moved on with them. They were not to "charge" the enemy but advance methodically behind the creeping artillery barrage. It was still dark when the advance began, and a heavy mist covered the area, the artillery bursts flashing cast an eerie glow, but as the sun came up, the mist did not dissipate, and as a result it was impossible to see very far.

Just as the boys were starting the attack, Pvt. Earnest Gurdner was cut down by shrapnel from German artillery. He was only a few feet from the starting point when killed. Thus, both Gurdner boys gave their lives within one month of each other and their mother would have two gold stars in her window back in Tennessee.

The Germans, of course, had suspected for several days that an attack was imminent; they just did not know when. According to later reports, the attack at that particular time was a complete surprise as most of the Germans were at breakfast. Another report, however, claimed that the time of the attack was well known since the enemy had shot down a British plane with the battle plans. Whatever the surprise factor, colored flares were soon sent skyward from the enemy positions signaling their machine guns and artillery that the Americans were coming. The air was filled with lead and artillery shells as our boys left the tape and proceeded toward the barbed wire.

The British plan of battle was for artillery rounds to begin falling in front of the advancing troops, closer and closer to the enemy, shielding the advancing Americans as they headed for the enemy positions. Every four minutes the artillery rounds would advance one hundred yards. Many of the shells fired were smoke rounds which, added to the mist, obscured the landscape more and more.

British Mark V tanks had also been brought forward, ten arriving in time for the assault by the 120th but twelve for the 119th were about one hour late. One enlisted man from each battalion had been designated to ride on a tank specifically to receive signals from his commander. Considering the limited visibility, the tanks were not as effective as planned but provided as much support as possible to the doughboys. Most of the tanks were destroyed by German artillery during the attack, but a few may have survived to help mop up Nauroy.

Over on the left the hard luck Twenty-seventh had kicked off one hour earlier in order to catch up to the Thirtieth, but the tanks there were also late in arriving. The Twenty-seventh suffered an even greater disadvantage because the rolling barrage in their front was about 1,000 yards distant instead of the prescribed 100 yards. The resulting gap meant that the Germans were not hindered by the bursting shells and could continue heavy enfilading fire into the ranks of the New Yorkers who hunkered down unable to move for much of the morning.

Back in the center the advance of the 119th and 120th continued but the former was held back by the same enfilade fire that was holding up the Twenty-seventh plus the standing orders to maintain contact with the New Yorkers. The formation thus created began to angle to the left of the line somewhat, with the 119th keeping touch with the stationary Twenty-seventh on their left and with their comrades in the 120th advancing on their right. This put the latter at the apex of the wedge which was created. The boys from Randolph and Durham Counties continued on with the eastern Davidson and Alamance County units following. Close behind them were the lads from Lexington.

Machine gun bullets were thick and murderous, but, owing to the mist and smoke, the enemy was also unable to see where to aim their pieces and hits were random. The tumultuous rattle and boom of the weapons was deafening and shouted orders were not heard. Men quickly became lost in the confusion, separated from their companions whom they could not see or hear even though they may have been only a few feet away. Men and tanks moved in and out of the mist like specters, appearing suddenly then disappearing again just as quickly.

At about 6:45 Pfc. Charlie Cook, another long time Company L boy, was killed by shell fire. Pfc. Harvey Ramsey and Pfc. Mickey Hopkins died at the same time in the same way.

Confusion was the order of the early part of the battle and the assault was in real danger of falling apart. Their inexperience in battle showed, but these were North Carolina boys, who had been taught from early boyhood that their forebears were "first at Bethel, farthest at Gettysburg, and last at Appomattox." Hardened on the border, trained at Camp Sevier and France to fight and think for themselves, the Tar Heels' officers and some noncoms gathered men around them and continued the advance toward a waiting enemy. The incessant tat-tat-tat of hundreds of machine guns and the resulting whine and dull thud of enemy lead striking dirt, metal, and human flesh was everywhere. Realizing that vision and hearing were severely impaired, the men adapted and moved on.

In the forefront of the attack Asheboro Company K's Ben Dixon was one of those officers who kept his boys moving. Wounded once, twice, then a third time Dixon inspired his men by his tenacity and kept them moving as they followed him into the hell before them. Then Dixon realized that his boys were moving too close to the artillery curtain. As he moved to redirect his men, a fourth bullet struck his throat ending his life. His last words were, "Go on, my boys, I am with you!" They went on. Only sixty-eight of the original 208 going into the battle would return unscathed.

Just behind Dixon's company, Captain Wallace Stone, Company L commander from West Main Street in Thomasville, also rallied his men shouting, "Follow me!" as the advance continued. R. O. Little and the rest of the company struggled on as the scattered men once more became a fighting unit. Slowly and steadily, these North Carolinians, with their heads bent toward the enemy as if leaning into the storm, advanced toward the machine guns, the *meinenwerfers*, and the Germans who used them. Several machine gun nests were overwhelmed as doughboys suddenly appeared out of the mist, surprising the doomed men who were the enemy. Much of the fighting was hand to hand, doughboys using bayonets, and rifle butts to take out the foe. Smoke bombs were tossed into German dugouts resulting in many Germans shouting "Kamerade" through their coughing spells. These men were taken prisoner.

The 115th Machine Gun Battalion, also of the Thirtieth Division, was advancing with the 120th. "I have seen men of Company A (the 115th MG) during the firing mount upon the parapet in front of their gun, refill it with water, lean over the top, and remedy a stoppage; stop and recheck their aim, or reset their aiming mark with as much ease and apparent self-control as an old woman changes her knitting needles."

As the advance continued the men realized that the artillery which was supposed to destroy the barbed wire and other defenses had indeed done the job in some sectors (the 119th's), but not in others (the 120th's). Tanks and heavy wire cutters finished the job where the artillery had not. Gradually the way was being cleared as the men slowly pushed ever forward. The way forward was over the top of the tunnel through which the waters of the St. Quentin Canal flowed and not through the water itself. Beyond the canal lay Bellicourt to the north and Nauroy to the east, the former assigned to the 119th and the latter to the 120th.

The Germans who thought the defenses could not be broken were falling back, grudgingly. Machine guns were silenced one at a time enabling the Americans to move forward a little further, then another and another. By 7:30, both regiments of the Sixtieth Brigade had crossed the canal, and the 119th on the left of the 120th were headed toward the outskirts of Bellicourt. The Hindenburg Line had been penetrated! The surprised Germans were falling back to the defensive positions that the two towns afforded in an effort to keep the Americans out.

From the beginning of trench warfare, the German tactic had been to bend but not break, allowing the Allied attacks to expend themselves then push them back with a well-timed counter attack. Knowing this, the training for the Americans had included mopping up activities which were vitally important to the success of the operation, but so eager were the Americans that units assigned to mopping up were caught up in the attack and continued onward. Consequently, as the doughboys passed over the canal, the Germans, true to their plan, emerged from the tunnel and began firing into the rear of the American ranks. The well-planned follow-up by the rest of the 120th and other regiments plus the Fifth Australians neutralized the threat, but only after heavy casualties were inflicted on the Americans.

First Battalion in the 120th was one of those assigned to mopping-up duties. Captain James Leonard's men (Company A) had followed the progress of the lead battalions and had seen some action. Recognizing that many men had lost direction he set up a command post virtually in the middle of the battlefield while enemy shells fell all around. Cooly, he assigned some of his company to those needing assistance. Slightly wounded, he organized other scattered men, over 150 of them, into a fighting unit and helped repulse an enemy counterattack. He was also able to direct men and officers to their assigned stations or units. Using captured machine guns and ammunition, even some enemy light artillery, he set up a perimeter to protect the flanks of the 120th.

As the battle progressed, Leonard moved his men forward. He would be commended for "acts of meritorious conduct" by the commanding general of the Thirtieth Division.

By 9:30 the Second and Third Battalions had crossed the canal, and the former had entered the southern part of Bellicourt, while the 119th held the northern sections. Pfc. Marvin Leonard (father of future MG Hubert M. Leonard) was dispatched to Headquarters, notifying them of the success of the 120th, the first such message to reach the commanders, causing instant elation in the rear areas. The advance continued and by 11:00 the Third Battalion was in the western part of Nauroy on the Le Catelet-Nauroy line where it halted in order to maintain contact with trailing battalions on their left. Resistance was isolated at this point, although the shelling from enemy artillery continued, while the men took cover on the streets of Nauroy and Bellicourt. Lead elements of both regiments moved forward past the town limits, but fell back slightly to consolidate and wait for the Australians.

Still pinned down on the left, the Twenty-seventh struggled against heavy odds to catch up. Impeded by enfilade fire, they advanced slowly, crossed the Hindenburg Line by 8:10 under the most hazardous conditions and were able to attain some of their objectives including the capture of Gouy north of Bellicourt. Far to the south the British had successfully taken the town of Bellenglise just across the canal on the east side.

Captain Leonard and his rag-tag group of men had also crossed the canal by this time. Asked if anyone had seen their commander, one of the men replied, "When I last saw the captain, he was chasing Bosch officers about in No Man's Land, beating them up with his cane because they would not give up their arms and field glasses for souvenirs."

By 11:30 the Australian Fifth Division had passed through the ranks of the doughboys. The exhausted men of the 120th watched as the "Aussies" marched over ground the Americans had taken and moved onward, keeping the Germans moving back. "Hi, Yanks, what in the hell are you quitting for?" shouted some of the Australians. Many of the Southern boys, thus goaded on by the Australians, just could not stay out of the fight and joined up with them to struggle on as the Allies consolidated their gains. All of these doughboys were recalled by noon on October 1 to their respective units.

Those Americans who had made it through the maelstrom were amazed that anyone had survived at all. The mist and smoke had finally lifted, and the day was clear, but smoke from burning equipment filled the air. Looking back at the terrain they had just fought over, they could see many bodies of men scattered throughout the area. Mules and horses were also killed, their wagons and equipment destroyed, overturned or otherwise rendered useless. Most of the tanks were twisted wrecks. In a war where gains had heretofore been measured in yards, the Americans had advanced almost two miles against the toughest defenses the Germans had to offer.

> Had they failed they could have been forgiven, but they did not fail, and the rays of the sun piercing the fog at 10:00 a.m. found the 120th on their objective, the only regiment in the whole attack who went through on time. The road was opened to the Australians, the lines had been broken, the defenses were ours. Our losses were grievous . . . Col. Sidney Minor.

Everywhere there were the men of the medical corps whose work had begun at the same time as the fighters, gathering up the wounded and dead. They had performed valiantly also, closely following or even among the advancing troops with their stretchers. Little aid other than to stop the wounded man from bleeding to death was given on the field of battle. The bearers quickly placed the injured on canvas stretchers then on ambulances for rapid transport to aid stations in the rear, then back again for more wounded.

Private George Land, a member of Company L, was designated as stretcher bearer for this battle and gave extraordinary service under fire. He was recommended for the Distinguished Service Cross, but not awarded. According to the reports, "Private Land elected to remain in the extreme forward areas, under constant fire, and superintended the work of evacuating the wounded. In this work he clearly rendered much service to the wounded and undoubtedly saved a great amount of suffering and probably several lives."

One of those wounded was R. O. Little. The defending Germans had begun lobbing gas artillery shells into the American ranks to try to stop the oncoming Americans. It may have been here that the lieutenant, against standing orders, but as resistance lessened, gave up his gas mask to a wounded soldier and was himself overcome by the toxic gas. The only account of this incident was given years later by the wounded soldier himself, who had come to Thomasville to thank the officer who had refused to leave him on the field of battle to die. No one knows his name.

Like the other wounded, Little was placed on a canvas stretcher then in an ambulance and rushed to the rear area for immediate treatment. At the aid station, he, along with other gas victims, was stripped of his clothing and rushed into a hot shower—the standard treatment for this type of injury. The efficiency with which the injured were treated was astounding—2,575 wounded were treated at aid stations, and 5,000 hot meals were served that day. The battlefield was cleared of all wounded by nightfall, an amazing statistic.

In the afternoon several large groups of dazed German prisoners were being marched toward the rear by the doughboys. Most of these men were incredulous that their impregnable fortress was now in possession of their enemy since they too had believed it could not be breeched. Many were openly glad that the war was over for them, and they gave no trouble to the lads of the Thirtieth.

The division captured 47 officers, 1,432 men of the ranks, and large amounts of weapons and ammunition. More importantly the Germans now knew that there was no defensive position between the Allies and the Rhine River that could hold the Allies back. Only the shattered remains of several German divisions could any longer put up a fight. One captured German officer was adamant in his belief that the line could not be breached. When finally convinced of the fact, he said in perfect English, "All is lost—there is nothing between you and the Rhine." Not that it was over by any means, for the Germans were determined to fight on; through pride or desperation, they would defend their fatherland.

From the battlefield, Lieutenant Little was transported by ambulance to a ship which eventually took him and others to a London hospital for treatment. His burned nostrils, mouth, and esophagus would heal somewhat, but Little was to spend the rest of the war in a London hospital and suffered lingering effects of the gas for the rest of his life.

Back home on October 16, in the local newspaper, Marvin Lambeth was reported as killed in action in the battle, but he was not dead. His right hip had been shattered by an artillery shell, and it was thought he could not survive the wound. On the day his parents were notified of his supposed death, Marvin's brother, Charlie, died from the effects of tuberculosis. One can only imagine the grief suffered by his parents.

View looking west from the Canal de St. Quentin, showing the ground over which the Americans had to fight to get to the canal, the strong point of the Hindenburg Line at Bellicourt. A demolished tank can be seen in the foreground. (Courtesy: NARA II) Below: Some of the 1479 Germans captured by the Thirtieth Division September 29, 1918. Operations continue by the 119th in the background. Nauroy is in the extreme distance. (Both Courtesy: NARA II)

Men of the Thirtieth Division scavenging machine gun belts after the battle.
The weapon at bottom left is a German *meinenwerfer*.
The canal is behind the men and Bellicourt is in the extreme distance.

The day after the breakthrough Lieutenant Colonel Pratt described the scene in his diary:

> Today, Monday, I went as far front as Bellicourt to inspect . . . the battlefield which was still being shelled by the Germans, and we were still having casualties. Dead and wounded were on the field, and it was all a realistic picture of the battle fields I had read about. It was a hard experience to see our men lying dead on the field, and while it was to be expected it did not ease the pain it caused me. There were also many dead Germans. Dead horses were scattered around and several guns were seen that had been knocked out of commission. There was a good deal of shelling of the area through which we passed . . .

The following is a list of KIAs of Company L according to a report by the company commander in January 1919.

- Pfc. Clarence I. Littlefield; Dalton, Kentucky; Sept. 29, 1918, 5:30; killed by shell fire while on tape awaiting orders to advance on enemy trenches in Hindenburg Line, Bellicourt, France; Old Hickory Cemetery #3 near Bellicourt, France.
- Pfc. Dewey M. Sanders; Biscoe, North Carolina; Sept. 29, 1918, 5:45; killed by machine gun fire while waiting to advance on enemy lines; Hindenburg Line, Bellicourt, France.
- Pfc. Ernest Gurdner; Johnson City, Tennessee (and Thomasville, North Carolina); Sept. 29, 1918; killed by shell fire about 1:00 a.m. while waiting to advance on enemy lines; Hindenburg Line, Bellicourt, France.
- Cpl. Lloyd C. Irvin; Huntersville, North Carolina; Sept. 29, 1918, 6:00; killed by shell fire while advancing on enemy trenches; Hindenburg Line, Bellicourt, France.
- Pvt. William H. Woods; hometown unknown; Sept. 29, 1918, 6:00; killed by shell fire about 6:00 a.m. while waiting to advance on enemy lines; Hindenburg Line, Bellicourt, France.
- Pvt. Jesse Slaven; Sept. 29, 1918, 6:10; killed by shell fire while waiting to advance on enemy lines; Hindenburg Line, Bellicourt, France.
- Pfc. Jessie L. Barkley; Woodleaf, North Carolina; Sept. 29, 1918, 6:25; killed by shell fire about 6:25 a.m. while advancing on enemy lines; Hindenburg Line, Bellicourt, France; Old Hickory Cemetery #3 near Bellicourt, France.
- George L. Broadway, Thomasville, North Carolina. Sept. 29, 1918; 0630; shell fire while advancing at Bellicourt.
- Sgt. Jess B. Jones; Mt. Airy, North Carolina; Sept. 29, 1918, 6:30; killed by machine gun fire while advancing on enemy trenches Hindenburg Line near Bellicourt.
- Pfc. Charlie Cook; Thomasville, North Carolina; Sept. 29, 1918, 6:45; killed by shell fire while advancing on enemy trenches, Hindenburg Line, Bellicourt, France
- Pfc. Harvey J. Ramsey; Albemarle, North Carolina; Sept. 29, 1918, 6:45; killed by shell fire while advancing on enemy trenches; Hindenburg Line; Bellicourt, France.
- Pfc. Mickey W. Hopkins; Thomasville, North Carolina; Sept. 29, 1918, 6:45; killed by shell fire while advancing on enemy trenches; Hindenburg Line; Bellicourt, France.
- Cpl. James H. Sloan; hometown unknown; Sept. 29, 1918, 7:00; killed by shell fire while advancing on enemy trenches; Hindenburg Line, Bellicourt, France.

In reading modern British or Australian accounts of the assault, it is difficult to determine sometimes that the Americans were involved in this battle at all, as it was a British operation. In British accounts, the Americans are barely even mentioned, and a similar account by Australians says that the Americans failed to meet their objectives, so the Australians had to help them as well as continue their own part of the plan—a blatant untruth. At least the Australians did give credit to some Americans for falling in as they passed through.

However the foreign powers see it, one thing remains uncontested—the 120th Regiment of the Sixtieth Brigade, American, of which Company L—Thomasville, Company K—Asheboro, and Company A—Lexington were a part, was in the spearhead of the assault that broke through the Hindenburg Line and the first to send back a report that the Hindenburg Line had been crossed. Whether or not the regiment was the first, second, or third to make that penetration, they were right on the mark in meeting their objectives. That means that the objective was met on time, a rarity in any battle.

Fortunately, at the time the attack by the Thirtieth Division was recognized as pivotal by the commander of the Australian Corps, General Sir John Monash, who wrote to General Read:

> The Corps Commander desires to make known to you his appreciation of the splendid fighting qualities of your division, and of the results accomplished in their part in breaking this formidable portion of the Hindenburg Line. It is undoubtedly due to the troops of this corps that the line was broken and the operations now going on made possible.
>
> The unflinching determination of these men, their gallantry in battle and the results accomplished are an example for the future. They will have their place in history and must always be a source of pride to your people.

The commander of all the British forces, General Sir Douglas Haig also praised the Thirtieth when he wrote:

> On the 29th of September, you took part with distinction in the great and critical attack which shattered the enemy's resistance in the Hindenburg Line, and opened the road to final victory. The deeds of the 27th and 30th American Divisions, who on that day took Bellicourt and Nauroy [the North Carolinians] and so gallantly

sustained the desperate struggle for Bony, [the New Yorkers] will rank with the highest achievements of the war. They will always be remembered by the British Regiments that fought beside you.

I rejoice at the success which has attended your effort and am proud to have had you under my command.[12]

Later he continued:

The enemy's defense in the last and strongest of his prepared positions had been shattered. The whole of the main Hindenburg Line passed into our possession and a wide gap was driven through such rear trench systems as had existed behind them.

The effect of the victory upon the subsequent course of the campaign was decisive. The threat to the enemy's communications was now direct and instant, for nothing but the natural obstacles of a wooded and well-watered countryside lay between our armies and Maubeuge.

Great as were the material losses the enemy had suffered, the effect of so overwhelming a defeat upon a morale already deteriorated was of even larger importance.[13]

General Pershing added:

The Second Army Corps, Major General Read commanding, with the 27th and 30th Divisions on the British Front, was assigned the task in cooperation with the Australian Corps of breaking the Hindenburg Line at Le Cateau, where the San Quentin Canal passes through a tunnel under a ridge. In this attack, carried out on the 29th of September and October 1st, the 30th Division speedily broke through the main line of defense and captured all of its objectives, while the 27th progressed until some of its elements reached Gouy.

---

[12] In actuality, the Second Corps was never under the direct command of the British or Australians. Although the relation between the Americans and the British was always "of the most cordial nature," the Americans were only "associated" with Brits.

[13] The Thirtieth Division in the World War, page 109.

That is, the 30th Division accomplished completely the task demanded of them, while the 27th Division fought gallantly but did not quite reach their objective.

The greatest tribute to the Thirtieth Division came from Charles Bean, Official Australian Correspondent when he wrote:

> Some day, when the full story of this battle can be told, the American people will thrill with pride in these magnificent troops upon whom a tremendous task fell. They were faced by the most formidable task that could be imposed upon them, the breaking of two double systems of the greatest defense line the Germans ever constructed. On the left of their attack there was some uncertainty regarding the situation and this increased the difficulty of their work; yet these troops, working under the enthusiasm of their high ideal, carried through their assaults, penetrated deeper than even had been intended, and delivered a blow which attracted the greatest part of the enemy's resistance. Beyond all question, they made it possible to break the defensive line in a position of the utmost importance to the Allied cause.

Some historians have placed this battle high above any other of the Great War. The January 23, 1920, edition of the *Masonic Journal* chronicled all of the regiments of the Thirtieth Division. Of the 120th it was stated, "Had been given the task of fighting the *only decisive battle* in the World War; that . . . the place of honor in this attack had been given the Fourth British Army; that the 30th Division . . . would attack in the center . . . that the 119th and 120th Infantry had been selected to do the job."

The Official History of the 118th Regiment echoed that sentiment.

CHAPTER TWELVE

REST AND REFITTING

~~~~

No. 225
GENERAL ROUTINE ORDERS
BY
FIELD-MARSHALL SIR DOUGLAS HAIG,
K.T., G.C.B. G.C.V.O., K.C.I.E.,
Commander-in-chief, British Armies in France

General Headquarters,
September 26th, 1918

ADJUTANT GENERAL'S BRANCH.
5014—Continental System of Time—Adoption of, throughout the British Army—The Continental system—of time—i.e., the 24 hour clock—will be brought into use throughout the British Army from midnight, 30th September/1st October, 1918.

The "time of origin," that is, the time at which a message or despatch is signed by the originator, will always be represented by four figures, the first two figures, 01 to 23, representing the hours from midnight to midnight, and the second two figures, 01 to 59, representing the minutes of the hour

~~~~

The YMCA and the RED CROSS

The importance of the Red Cross and the YMCA cannot be overstated. Charged with caring for the wounded and the dead they were everywhere they needed to be, even among the advancing troops. Accounts from many sources, including the wounded themselves, give testament to the unflinching service given to the men of the AEF whenever and wherever needed. In addition, many of the staff of the YMCA volunteered as stretcher bearers, risking their lives when they could have stayed safely in the rear. These men served their fellow man without hesitancy under the most dangerous conditions. Their service was highly praised by the men and never forgotten by them.

~~~~

After Bellicourt, General Haig's BEF faced the German Eighteenth and Second Armies on a wide front near Montbrehain. On October 1, the Second Corps, American, was pulled back for rest and refitting to the Le Mesnil/ Herbecourt area, but the 118th remained at the front. General Order 33, October 1, issued congratulations for the "courage, fortitude, and devotion displayed" in the recent battle. "There is a deep and keen regret for the gallant comrades who have gloriously died" it went on, and "the Division may do to the fullest extent possible its share in bringing about the early success of the great cause in which they have fallen." It was signed by Major General Lewis, commander of the Thirtieth Division.

Refitting, of course, meant replacements for those who had been lost in battle one way or another. New troops were arriving daily from the States and a few were assigned to the 120th as needed. By this time in the war, the new men were all draftees who had been rushed through basic training. Sadly, some did not even know how to fire a rifle because their stateside training had been so rudimentary.

Longer periods of rest were normal but by this time the Germans were back on their heels, and the opportunity presented meant that the division was called back into action only four days after leaving the front. Therefore the ranks were not fully filled by replacements, but the American units were still larger than any of the BEF units—an American regiment had about twice as many men as a British equivalent. According to 1st Lt. Joe Cecil of Company A, "We hope[d] to come out for a rest in a few days, or right away. We were pulled out for a rest once before, walked 10 miles one way, rested the next, then walked back over the same trail and went to fighting. So there is really no rest."

As the prisoners had said, the enemy had no prepared positions for defense after the Hindenburg Line. There would be no more static trench warfare but that did not mean the Germans had given up. They were defending their homeland and were just as formidable a foe as ever in the front lines. Mostly they were a proud fighting unit and their struggle at this point was to keep the Allies out of Germany. (After the armistice they were welcomed home as heroes for doing just that.) For the Allies every chance given must be taken if the war were to be brought to an early end. The Axis commanders already knew by this time that they could not hold out much longer. The Allies also knew this and were determined to keep the pressure on the Germans to end the war as soon as possible.

The Kaiser was also on shaky ground and would eventually be forced to abdicate and go into exile. The Allies could not let up yet since the enemy must be beaten into submission, and treaty favorable to the victors must be assured. The fight had to be taken to the Germans and be maintained on a wide front for a successful conclusion to the conflict.

Sometime around the first of October, Colonel Wade Phillips was transferred to the Judge Advocates Office where he was to handle claims by citizenry over damage by the war. He was reluctant to go, but orders are orders. Also, Captain James A. Leonard was promoted to major and given command of First Battalion. Luther Propst took command of Company A since Lieutenant Joe Cecil had been named Transport Officer and placed in charge of food supplies for the battalion. With R. O. Little taken to the hospital in London, 1st Lt. Gordon Gillespie, from Memphis, Tennessee, rushed to the front lines on October 6 to replace him. The time spent in Tincourt was so brief that many new men assigned to the Thirtieth Division arrived too late to report and were assigned elsewhere, thus the division was once again going back into battle under strength.

CHAPTER THIRTEEN

THE FINAL BATTLES

The Battle of Montbrehain, as it was later called, started off badly for the Allies. The Thirtieth had been called back to the sector they had just liberated to continue the drive eastward toward Montbrehain and the Selle River. The land here was much different from the shell-pocked landscape to the west which the two divisions had traversed on September 29. This was beautiful country where trees were still standing and villages were not piles of rubble. Static trench warfare was a thing of the past and with the coolness of autumn definitely in the air, the Americans moved out to finish the job.

The Fifty-ninth Brigade had remained at the front so their two regiments—the 117th and 118th were to spearhead the initial assault. These were the South Carolinians mostly. The 118th had little difficulty moving closer into the front lines, but the 117th was far behind on the left, so the operations of October 5-7 were meant to bring the 117th abreast of the 118th. Positioned about one kilometer in the rear, the 117th attempted to advance under heavy enemy fire, which resulted in chaotic engagements that isolated some platoons from their commanders. Elements of the 117th were virtually surrounded by the enemy. There were even rumors, fortunately untrue, that one platoon had been wiped out. At the end of the day, however, the commanders felt that sufficient gains had been made so that the main assault could be launched on October 8.

To the 118th regiment was added First Battalion (which included the Lexington boys) of the 120th in reserve. At 0510 on October 8, with the British on the left and on the right, the Fifty-ninth Brigade moved out on schedule. The Sixtieth Brigade, the 120th, and 119th regiments were to follow the advancing lead elements in support. This attack was planned similarly to the assault just ten days prior. A rolling barrage preceded the doughboys as they pushed toward the town of Brancourt-le-Grand, but this time the artillery was not as effective and, once again, the British did not take their objectives on schedule. The assault was not completely successful, and the doughboys were halted before reaching Brancourt, the primary objective. At 1100 hours after the addition of Company D (Louisburg) of the 120th, strengthened the front, the town was taken. The enemy still commanded the heights, and every move of the Americans was severely contested throughout the day. As night fell, the men dug in while at the same time Company C (Henderson) of the 120th was brought forward to plug the gap between the Americans and the British, thus consolidating the lines.

On the left, the 117th Infantry advanced on Premont on schedule; but because the British had not, a gap was opened in the lines. Companies A and B of the 120th were sent to plug the gap and consolidate the lines. Thus strengthened, the primary objective of Brancourt-le-Grand was taken about 0730. Brancourt, the contingent objective, fell at 0810, and the doughboys moved toward Premont at 1800. During the afternoon hours, a spectacular charge on the enemy front by British cavalry resulted in a spectacular failure, although it was gallantly done. Men on horseback using pistols and carbines were no match for well-concealed machine guns commanding the heights.

After a hectic night in which new orders were issued by headquarters, carried back to the front on a moonless night, with no light of any kind, and distributed to the front lines with no time to spare, the 118th adjusted their front and was ready to move out again before daybreak. This feat ranks high on the list of the extraordinary accomplishments by the Old Hickory Division. At 0520, with the Sixtieth Brigade in reserve, the 118th moved out. At this time, Second and Third Battalions of the 120th, having been used as support, were to filter through the 118th to continue the assault. First Battalion was reattached to the Second and Third, making the 120th Regiment whole again. The order of battle was as follows: The 119th Infantry (the eastern North Carolinians) on the left with Second Battalion and Third Battalion abreast, First Battalion in reserve. On the right, the 120th Infantry, First Battalion and Second Battalion abreast, Third Battalion in reserve. Thus, the Lexington and Thomasville boys of the 120th were back in the front lines for the second time in ten days, the "Blues" in reserve.

Over in England, Robert Little, recovering but still not healed from his wounds, celebrated his thirtieth birthday on October 10. He spent some of the time reflecting on his family in Thomasville. Back in August, while in Belgium, he had bought a lace-trimmed card at the YMCA and sent it to his youngest son, Max, whom he had only seen a few times. The toddler was two years old on September 18 and didn't know much about his father. It would be several more months before he would be able to get acquainted with his dad. His oldest son, also named Robert, was nine, Paul was six, and Carson was four. All three of them had good memories of their dad. He wrote to Maud regularly, mostly using picture postcards, the fad of the day. (It is from these picture postcards that Robert's travels can be determined since he was now separated from his unit.)

On the battlefront, early on the morning of October 10, the doughboys moved out, but part of the Third Battalion quickly became lost, veered to the right, and ironically captured the primary objective of Becquigny. While occupying the town, another platoon from the Third Battalion was sent to the British and helped them capture Bohain. In this confusing battle, therefore, the boys of Company L were involved in some of the most important achievements of the day's battles.

Over on the left, the 117th depleted by the withdrawal of the 120th's First Battalion was now faced with a large gap in their lines. However, by 1300, the 117th reached its objective against strong resistance.

The intermediate objectives of the 117th and 118th, having been reached a little behind schedule, the 120th leapfrogged the 118th and continued to push toward the town of Vaux-Andigny, heavily fortified by the enemy. Little resistance was encountered until the outskirts of the town, but the gap on the right, again because the British were pinned down, exposed the Second Battalion to flanking fire. Despite this, the 120th entered the western edge of Vaux-Andigny and passed through to the other side. The situation there being unsupported, the 120th was forced back with heavy casualties as night fell. Patrols were sent out during the night to establish contact with the British on the right and the 119th on the left which had met little resistance and was far ahead of the 120th.

The final objective for this battle was the Selle River, and the 119th had almost reached that point. However, since the other units, including the 120th and the British, had met stiff resistance, the 119th was halted at St. Souplet/St. Benin on the banks of the Selle. This was a wise move since a crossing of the river by only one regiment would surely result in its annihilation. Better wait for the others to catch up. Leapfrogging once again the 118th passed through the ranks of the 120th for the push to the river, and the First Battalion of the 120th was attached in reserve to the 118th. The advance of the 118th was strongly contested by the enemy, and little headway was made toward the river. The 120th (less First Battalion) was still in possession of Vaux-Andigny and the immediate area, so the 118th was able to make some small gains in that direction. Once again the British were not advancing at all due to heavy fire from the heights to their right and front. That being the case the advance to the Selle on that front also was halted short of the objective. That afternoon, Second Battalion, 120th Infantry, was sent to close the gap with the British which was done successfully.

During the night of October 11/12, the Twenty-seventh Division was brought forward to relieve the Sixtieth Brigade in the front lines. Still hoping to cross the Selle, the British commanders were prepared to make an all-out effort and push the enemy further toward their homeland. Reconnaissance patrols and aircraft revealed that the Germans were massing for a determined stand at the Selle, holding the high ground and with a clear field of fire. With Allied artillery not in position because of the rapid advance over rough terrain and with the Germans still holding the high ground, HQ wisely decided to wait until the troops could be consolidated and the situation be better assessed. The net result was a period of relative quiet considering what the men had been through in the last few days.

The fighting from October 7 through October 11, collectively called the "Battle of Montbrehain" had resulted in a gain of over sixteen square miles of territory being taken from the enemy who had put up a stubborn and determined resistance. Many towns and smaller villages had been liberated and a large number of prisoners freed. It was obvious from the tactics displayed that the Germans were fighting a rear guard action, necessitated by the loss of the Hindenburg Line several days before. In addition, the economic, political, and military situation for the Germans was desperate, but for the men on the front lines, the fighting would go on.

Aerial reconnaissance on October 14 showed that the Selle River, not much more than a large stream, was the enemy's last true line of defense since the land beyond the river was poorly suited for holding the British, Americans, and French back. Therefore, the best troops the Germans had left were poured into defense on the east side of the waterway, with orders to keep the Allies on the west side at all costs. They were also ordered to fight to the last man in defense of the fatherland.

On October 15, Corporal Herbert Parks and Private Harry Cardwell were promoted to sergeant. Harrison Sullivan, Company L, was promoted from private to corporal. Preparations for a planned attack to cross the river continued as a cold rain fell relentlessly.

By this time the fame of the two American divisions had become well known so the British Fourth Army, to which the Americans were attached, was once again the spearhead of the big push aimed at crossing the Selle. Extra artillery was added, and American tanks were attached to the Twenty-seventh Division and the Thirtieth, which had joined their New York brethren on the front lines on the night of October 17/18. The weather continued cold and rainy, poor conditions for any sort of military action, but the Fifty-ninth Brigade began the attack as ordered with the Sixtieth following in close support. Executing a curious maneuver, the plan was for the New York Division, the Twenty-seventh, once again on the left of the Thirtieth beginning at 0530 to advance rapidly, keeping in touch with the Sixtieth Brigade on their right, who in turn, would hinge on the British division which had decided it would remain stationary until 1000.

At the appointed hour the New Yorkers stepped off keeping contact with the 119th and moved forward through the 118th without artillery support toward Ribeauville and, this time as planned, once again outdistanced the 120th. At 1100 American artillery laid down a barrage in which several rounds fell short compelling the men to fall back several hundred yards. Consequently the 119th's flank was exposed, so patrols were sent out to make contact with the 120th which was accomplished, as the rain continued to pelt down.

The 120th, having been ordered to pass through the 117th, whether or not the latter had attained their objectives, had dutifully pushed off in concordance with the 119th at 0530 that morning; First and Second Battalions were in front, and the Third was in support. Even though they had only the use of two machine guns captured from the enemy, two platoons from the 105th Engineers were added to Third Battalion, which had been so decimated since September 29. Concealed by a heavy fog, little resistance was encountered until about 1030 when the mist lifted, affording the enemy excellent visibility who then opened up with heavy machine gun fire and artillery from well-concealed positions. The Americans, caught in the open, were forced to return to their original lines until about 1800, when another determined push extended their front lines near Arbre Guernon where they rested on arms for the night.

The Germans had begun resorting to booby traps to hold the Americans back. Although this tactic had been employed on the battlefield before, this time the 105th Engineers had found three hundred pounds of explosive the Germans had placed in the church steeple at St. Martin Riviere, rigged to blow when anyone were to kneel at the altar inside. The engineers successfully dismantled the trap with no casualties. (Joseph Hyde Pratt)

During this action, the last member of Company L from Thomasville to lose his life on the field of battle made the supreme sacrifice. While he slept from exhaustion under a haystack, Harrison Sullivan, newly promoted to corporal, was killed, probably by a sniper. Sullivan was a member of Reformed Church on Salem Street in Thomasville. He was truly a boyish-looking soldier, age twenty-seven, who, out of uniform, would have fit right in at the corner drugstore having a laugh with his chums. His boyish looks, however, hid the fact that he was a brave soldier. Like Hammett Harris, Haymore Westmoreland, the Gurdners, and the rest before him, these boys gave their lives for an ideal which was to them more important than life—the security of freedom—the American ideal.

Next day, October 19 at 0530, the brigade was ordered to take the town of Mazingheim which was accomplished by 1000. Heavy fire from every hedge and bunker stopped the brigade in their tracks until Australian artillery fire raked the area. Newly assigned 1st Lt. Gordon Gillespie was killed while leading his men in this final action. Sgt. William S. Wilson, in a letter to *The Dispatch*, related a darker side of battle when he wrote:

> As we advanced, there came from a dugout about ten or twelve Germans with their hands up. Someone cried out, "Take them prisoner!" Another yelled, "Kill them, for they killed our officer." And take it from me, there was few spared of that bunch.

On this last day of battle, Sgt. Clyde Shelton earned the Distinguished Service Cross by his actions in the enemy front, to wit:

> In command of a platoon was ordered to push a Lewis gun out on the right flank of the First Battalion which had been held up by heavy fire east of MAZINGHEIM, FRANCE. In order to accomplish his task it was necessary to advance through a hedge and wire fence clearly within view of the enemy and under heavy fire. Sergeant Shelton held his platoon and then himself went forward, cutting a wide opening in the barrier permitting of easy passage for his patrol and then pushed further into the open to establish the line. By his gallant work Sergeant Shelton facilitated *[sic]* the progress of the patrol, reducing the chance of casualties to the minimum and

enabling the patrol to render the greatest benefit to the unit it was supporting by driving out persistent enemy gunners.

Other members of the platoon, Pvt. Ollie Cranford, Cpl. Ocie A. Bedgood, Pvt. Ed Fricks, Pvt. Ollie Cranford, and Pvt. Riley Rawlings were recommended but not awarded.

In the same letter cited above Wilson tells another side of the peculiarities of this war.

> One day when we were advancing, or rather we went to relieve a division, those we were to relieve were held up on account of a machine gun nest. One of our sergeants walked down the trench and asked those we were to relieve why they were kept there. The reply was that a nest of machine guns was out in front. The sergeant laughed and told them to stand up, whereupon he jumped out of the trench without a gun and waved his hand in the direction of the Germans and out came six of them. The Americans feared nothing.

This also points out the fact that, at this time of the war, due to the loss of the Hindenburg defenses, the Germans knew the end was near. No sense getting killed when all is lost anyway.

Orders were received to consolidate before moving onward but at the same time new orders were received that the British would relieve the doughboys of the Thirtieth Division. It was estimated that if they had not been relieved, they would have crossed the Selle River and achieved their objective in one more hour. Reluctantly in some cases, by 2358 that evening the brigade fell back as the Tommies took over the operation.

Also very well aware that the end was near, but anticipating a return to battle, the division retired to Tincourt for refitting and rest. During this time Wallace Stone was acting battalion commander, awaiting the arrival of a replacement for Wade Phillips who had been pulled out to serve on the war reparations staff because of his civilian occupation as an attorney. He was reluctant to go and tried to decline the position, but finally went saying that orders are orders and must be obeyed. Captain Samuel Boddie was promoted to major and took Phillip's place as commander of the third Brigaide.

New men were added to the regiment, but they were never to see battle. The men who had been through so much were rather aloof to the new men, since the latter would never experience the horrors and exhilaration of war. Not that it was intended, but the veterans were a breed unto themselves, and the rookies would never receive their baptism of fire after which their admission into the group would have been accepted.

It was fortunate that the Thirtieth never did return to battle because one of the most horrible acts of war ever committed occurred on the last day of the war. At the last moment before the guns fell silent, commanders were still ordering men to die in battle knowing the exact hour of the cessation of hostilities had already been determined. At 0500 on November 11, 1918, the Germans signed an armistice agreement on a railroad car outside of Paris. The agreed-upon time was at 1100, that day. The news was flashed immediately to all fronts and was received by all commanders.

Pershing, for his part, did communicate the fact of the armistice, but incredibly left out any orders as to whether to continue operations or not. Unbelievably, commanders ordered an attack to take a little more land or another town, which they could have walked into a few hours later. In some cases this action was taken for glory to the regiments, or because the unit had never tasted battle and wanted to do so, or had been repulsed at a particular point and this was the last chance to take that place in battle. Stenay, the last town taken by the Americans was attacked and occupied because the commander of the Eighty-ninth Division, Major General William M. Wright, knew there were bathing facilities in that town; and he wanted his men to be able to take a bath. A single German artillery round made sure that twenty Americans would never get that bath. They were killed outright, many others wounded.[14]

Whatever the reasons, the actions by some officers on all fronts was inexcusable, even criminal. Some commanders flatly refused to attack but were ordered by higher brass to do so. American, British, and French units charged into the defensive positions of the Germans who had no choice but to defend themselves. It was estimated that ten thousand Allied casualties were the result of operations during the six hours from the time the armistice was signed at 0500.

---

[14]   The Eighty-first "Wildcat Division," who had recently arrived in France and made up mostly of North Carolina men, was involved in this last attack and lost several men. In some newspaper articles of the day, the nickname "Wildcat" is sometimes mistakenly applied to the Thirtieth Division.

Commanders of the Thirtieth did not have to make such a decision, but some commanders of other units were adamant and did not attack as ordered.

Officially, the last man to die in battle was an Englishman, who was killed at 1059; but an American, Henry M. Gunther, from Baltimore was killed at the same time. After fighting with his unit all morning, he alone charged a German machine gun nest. The defenders tried to wave him back, but Gunther ignored them, and the Germans took one last American life.

One minute later the guns fell silent.

At the moment of the end of the war, November 11, 1918, men stopped in their tracks, and an eerie calm fell over the battlefields. The Germans laid down their weapons and no one moved—for a moment. Then one mighty roar arose from the throats of the Allies as a great cheer went up all along the front. Dancing, singing, and shouting, the allied soldiers celebrated unabashedly while the Germans stared in shocked disbelief. It was over! After four of the bloodiest years in the history of man, it was over!

In rear areas also, the men celebrated. In fact the whole world, at least the allied side, celebrated. The armistice was only a cessation of hostilities while the two sides negotiated the peace, but even though both sides were still armed and could have carried on the conflict, Germany and the central powers were beaten. How to secure the peace would occupy the world stage for more than six months until the harsh Treaty of Versailles was signed.

In the daily log for Company L, the following notation was made for November 11, 1918: "Bn. carried out drill schedule in morning. Afternoon—Holiday per Regt'l. Orders.

James W. Jenkins
Major Comdng.

First Battalion's daily log stated, "Bn left at 8:00 for field problem but returned as it was call[ed] off by the CO and the troops were excuse[d] for the balance of the day. Words were recd by all ranks with great joy of the signing of the armistice by the German delegates.

W. L. Propst 1st Lt. Inf Act Adjt."

That the battles fought by the Thirtieth and Twenty-seventh Divisions from September 27, 1918, were decisive in the outcome of the war cannot be denied. The campaigns fought by these North and South Carolina boys were like a spear aimed directly at the heart of the German war machine and therefore Germany herself. Testimony from both sides laid claim to the fact that the advances made by these Americans caused irreparable damage to the still formidable defense of the Germans. Nothing could hold the Americans back, and the road to final victory was aided immensely by them.

HEADQUARTERS 120th INFANTRY
AMERICAN EXPEDITIONARY FORCES
FRANCE JANUARY 26th, 1919

At the first formation the following will be read to all rank of your organization.

(a) What Regiment first broke through the Hindenburg Line on 29th of Sept?

The 120th INFANTRY

(b) What was the only regiment that went through to its objective and on time?

The 120th INFANTRY

(c) What regiment captured the towns of Bellicourt and Nauroy?

The 120th INFANTRY

(d) Remember that your regiment was not assisted in your mission on the 29th by any infantry troops.

(E) Remember that your regiment has nothing to explain or to apologize for.

(F) Your accomplishments are a continual source of pride to your Commanding Officer, and he knows that no officer or man will, regardless of conditions, permit their regiment to be second to any in the American army.

BY ORDERS OF COLONEL MINOR
John O. Walker,
Major Inf, U. S. A.
Operations Officer

CHAPTER FOURTEEN

TIME TO GO HOME?

~~~~~

We left the British a few weeks later, moved to the S. O. S.
area near Le Mans where we had our first experience with the
American Army.—Col. Sidney Minor

~~~~~

Since the armistice had been signed, it was time to go home, or so the men
thought. The Second Corps was not part of the army of occupation which
stayed on the front lines, so home was the logical next step. But somewhere
in the upper echelons, the brass was deciding how to get the doughboys
home again at a minimum cost to the U.S. government. Their reasoning was
an astounding example of typical army wisdom—the men would go home
in reverse order of the way they arrived. In other words, those who arrived
first would go home last; those who arrived last would go home first. In some
cases men arriving on one day would board another ship for home a day or
two later.

The plan had its merits, since the units which had been there the longest were
furthest from the point of departure and would have to march through the
newcomers to board the transports. They were not really that far from the
ports, though, so how that arrangement was formulated is still a mystery. The
pages of history are silent as to how this logic by the higher brass was well
received or not. Probably not. Surely, the cry of so long ago by the boy from
Company K on the border in 1916, "I WANT TO GO HOME!" was shouted
again to the heavens by many of the doughboys.

What is for certain is that the days were filled with momentary excitement such as mule races between the two divisions, the Twenty-seventh and Thirtieth, boxing matches and song and dance theater performed by the men themselves. The rest of the time was filled with sheer boredom. In an effort to keep the men busy, training also continued as target practice and army drills were scheduled day after day.

It was also a time when, in an effort to keep discipline, minor offenses occurred, which would never have taken place during the recent war. Disobeying, ignoring orders, or talking back to the sergeants was the most common occurrence. One soldier was sentenced to ten days at hard labor for his offense, which, on appeal, the verdict was upheld but the sentence suspended.

One piece of unfinished business that had to be finalized was that of Bennett Williams's absence from the company from February 12 to July 18. Williams had fought in every battle with his comrades and had come through unscathed, but on January 26, 1919, he was brought up on charges of violating the Sixty-first Article of War. His guilty plea was accepted, and he was sentenced to two months at hard labor to be carried out at the company station.

During this time Wallace Stone, whose luggage had been lost on September 29, sent requests to battalion to help find it. Worn out shoes were sent to be repaired and were lost. The shoes that were returned were not the ones sent and were in worse shape than before or were not even matched pairs. In February 1919, it was reported that a fire bucket was also stolen and mysteriously replaced a few days later. An answer to a request from Headquarters, by Stone stated, "There are no men in the enlisted personnel of this organization who desire to remain in France as Mess Sergeants, Cooks, Typists, Stenographers, Clerks, Orderlies, or Auto Mechanics."

On February 24, 1919, the 120th was assembled as Sergeant Clyde Shelton, Company L, was awarded the Distinguished Service Cross. (Apparently the request by Captain Stone dated January 23, for a reduction in rank to corporal for Shelton had been denied.)

Also during the wait, men who had been transferred to other duties for one reason or another were recalled. Sergeants Wilson and Stratton cited above had been sent to officers' training but were returned at the same rank to Company L since they were no longer needed as officers. On March 18, 1919, Sergeant Paul Green, who had been loaned to Third Corps as an instructor was returned to Company L. Benedetto Gannacone, a newly arrived lad from New Castle,

Pennsylvania, was discharged in Europe so that he could visit his parents in Naples, Italy, where he was born. In doing so he agreed that he would pay his own way back to the United States.

The days had to be filled somehow so regular drill was held almost every day, and the men soon grew tired of the routine. The armistice, after all, was only a truce, so Germany could theoretically rearm if they were able. In fact, in June of 1919, the Germans expressed their disgust at being excluded from negotiating the peace and signaled their intent to resume hostilities. Allied troops were put on alert. It all came to naught, though, and the peace talks proceeded without them, nor did the Germans rearm.

And so it went—mundane days and mundane nights with a few furloughs. Meanwhile, the boys moved ever closer to the coast of France and the ships home. Company A moved from St. Souplet then Tincourt, then Montigny, Segrie, Le Mans to St. Nazaire on the coast of France. Company L also assembled at St. Souplet on October 20, then Tincourt on October 23. From there to Beaucourt, Vernie, La Bazoge, Le Mans, and St. Nazaire, by design arriving a few days behind the rest of the 120th.

In the home states of most of the men from the Thirtieth, the public eagerly awaited the arrival of their men. For months the newspapers were filled with speculation as to when they would return. First one day then another was announced and then canceled. The war department issued speculation then rescinded it. The newer recruits, mostly draftees, were already home and receiving the thanks of their neighbors, but they had not been gone very long, just a few weeks. The men of Company L and Company A had really been gone since September 1916 when they left for El Paso so long ago. Nothing, however, could rush the army's schedule and the wait continued.

The anticipated parade through major cities was also canceled by the war department which cited lack of funds. The troops were to return home and be mustered out immediately. Mayor Frank R. McNinch of Charlotte led a delegation to Washington to reason with Secretary of War Baker in an effort to secure a welcome home for the doughboys. They were successful primarily because local organizations had raised enough money for the celebrations so that it would not cost the federal government as much. The plan was for the 120th to land at Wilmington, North Carolina, assemble at Camp Jackson, South Carolina, board trains for Charlotte, return to Jackson, and be mustered out. The

119th was to parade in Wilmington and the 113th Artillery in Raleigh before going home.

But when would they be home? On February 2, it was reported that they had started the movement home and were soon to be at Brest, France, for the transport, but at this time they were still at La Bazoge and Segrie awaiting the next station at Le Mans. Like a large funnel, the men were coming from all over France to the ports to go home. The wait seemed interminable.

After his wounds had healed enough R. O. Little was discharged from the hospital and billeted near London. He still had discomfort in his lungs and windpipe, but it was thought that after a time, he would heal completely. He was able to travel all over the United Kingdom by rail visiting places he never would have had the opportunity to see before or after the war. He saw the highlands of Scotland and Belfast in Ireland and all of the touristy sights in London along with some new friends he had made. But he longed to go home and the wait for him too seemed never to end.

Meanwhile, wounded men were being returned to the States from England on a priority basis. Some wounds were severe, and these men were admitted to hospitals all over the east coast. Others' wounds were considered not life threatening, and they were sent home. In one of his postcards home, postmarked December 10, from London, Robert said, "I believe we are about ready to go " . . . On January 20, 1919, a cablegram was delivered to Maude Little, R. O.'s wife, saying only "Am Sailing today Robert Little." Exactly what transport they were on is not recorded, but they probably landed at Charleston, South Carolina, and were taken to Fort McPherson's excellent hospital facility in Atlanta for a final checkup before being sent home. It is possible, however, that his homeward route was through New York since he brought home postcards from Gettysburg, Pennsylvania, as well as some from Fort McPherson.

Although this photograph is not identified, it appears to be the day room at
the London hospital where R. O. Little convalesced. It was taken on Christmas,
judging by the decorations, the same time he would have been there.
(Courtesy: Patsy Henderson)

Finally, on February 19, 1919, it was reported that Robert had returned and
was with his family "in the northern part of the city." His last stop in the
military had been at Camp Lee, Virginia, where he received his discharge.
"The following named Officers are honorably discharged from the service of
the United States for the convenience of the Government . . . their services
being no longer required." Fourth on the list of fourteen was "Little, Robert O.
1st Lieutenant, Infantry." He received $60 from the United States Army at the
time of his separation.

Back in France, as the men prepared to go home a memorandum dated March
3, 1919, listed the officers of Company L as follows: Capt. Wallace B. Stone,
Thomasville, NC; 1st Lieutenant Thomas B. Marshall, Columbia, SC; and
2nd Lieutenant James G. Mackin, Montross, NY. Commanding the 120th
was Colonel Sidney Minor, Lt. Colonel Don Scott, second in command; Major
James Leonard, First Battalion; Major Hilliard Comstock, Second Battalion;
and Major James W. Jenkins, Third Battalion.

A final accounting of the valiant men who went "over there" is as follows:

No. of original brought overseas	Officers	6
	Men	243
No. of original who are still with organization	Officers	2
	Men	152
No. of original returned to the States	Officers	1
	Men	0
No. who are now in hospitals or otherwise separated and dropped from the rolls	Officers	3
	Men	91

Toward the end of March 1919 real progress could be seen in getting the men of the 120th home again. Orders were issued for the loading of men requiring twelve copies with names, ranks, and destinations. It was all done very efficiently by the quartermaster corps having had months of practice. One last hitch delayed the regiment for a few days—the change of destination from Wilmington to Charleston—then, finally, in almost the same arrangement as the trip over, the regiment was sent home.

On March 28, the boys from Company A along with Headquarters, supply, and others, about 2,500 men, boarded the Powhatan[15] and set sail. On April 1, the rest of the men including Company L embarked on the Martha Washington, about three thousand men. Some of these were replacements from all over the United States who had never even been to the Carolinas except for the military, but there was no rancor about their destination or their immediate future. They were now part of what some called the finest fighting unit in the American army.

(In Lexington's *The Dispatch* dated April 5, 1919, the editor duly noted the reported departure from France of the Powhatan. Just below that article appeared the small headline "For Mayor—Major James A. Leonard.")

The trip home for both transports was uneventful, of course, since there was no fear of German U-boats, plus the weather was beautiful. The troops were often

---

[15] Curiously, the *High Point Enterprise*, citing the Associated Press, listed the names of the transports as the Huron and the Madawaska. At the Division of Archives in Raleigh, two ships with these names are pictured at Charleston harbor purportedly bringing home the Thirtieth Division with documentation included. The preponderance of information, however, is that the ships were those listed in this narrative.

entertained on board by the band which just as they had done throughout overseas duty. The men found many ways to amuse themselves too. Crowded as it was on board there was always something going on on deck in the way of amusing themselves. The spirits of the homeward bound men soared the nearer to home they came, and the riggings of the ship were filled daily with happy men.

Men of the 30th Division on board the Martha Washington on their way home from the war in France. They are crowding the deck and rigging observing a sporting event. Instead of the customary wool khakis the men are wearing blue denim issued to them for the voyage. [N. C. Archives, Col. Joseph Hyde Pratt Collection

After a pleasant voyage of about two weeks, the Powhatan reached port in the morning of April 10, 1919, whereupon the troops debarked and took trains for Camp Jackson, near Columbia, South Carolina. Two days later the Martha Washington landed and followed the rest of the boys into Camp Jackson. Whole again, the Thirtieth Division prepared to muster out.

Upon debarking from the Martha Washington, General Faison, commander of the Sixtieth Brigade was asked by a reporter for a statement. "We were called to France to fight. We kicked hell out of the Hun. We came home," was his terse reply.

"The confusion over when and where the 119th Regiment would parade continued up until the very last moment. The Eastern North Carolina men were originally to march in Wilmington, but the mayor there claimed that they did not have enough time to prepare, and the event was canceled. When that was made public, Charlotte volunteered to host them along with the 120th. Eventually, the 119th paraded in Columbia, South Carolina, on April 5, 1919, then mustered out one week later. Elements of the unit also paraded in Goldsboro and Fayetteville, North Carolina. The 113th Field Artillery, which was separated from the Thirtieth upon arriving in France, had a grand parade down Hillsborough Street from the Capitol building in Raleigh.

There was no confusion as to where the 120th was to parade, never had been. Charlotte formed hasty committees of welcome headed by Mayor McNinch to honor the inbound heroes. Hasty, yes, but the planning was so thorough that not a single detail was left undone. Each county represented by the original North Carolina Third Brigade was asked to set up a booth of welcome for their men; women from the counties were recruited to provide food and gifts for them, and newspaper articles detailed where the public would be best able to find their loved ones.

On the appointed day, Wednesday, April 16, 1919, the troops boarded early trains from Camp Jackson, formed up and marched down Tryon Street in Charlotte. Hundreds of thousands lined the route waving flags and cheering. Leading the procession was Major General Samson L. Faison and Colonel Sidney W. Minor who, according to protocol, mounted the reviewing stand as the rest of the regiment passed in review. With the officers on the platform were Senator Lee Overman, Mayor McNinch, and Governor Thomas W. Bickett. Other than a few showers in the afternoon, the whole affair went without a hitch. It was the biggest, grandest parade of its type ever held in the state of North Carolina.

Lieutenant Little probably did not march with his old unit in the parade, but he may have gone to Charlotte. Having already been discharged from active service, he would not have been authorized to march with the men. Maybe some of his comrades saw him and enticed him to march on with them, but that is speculation. He was probably in the crowds and reunited with the men of his unit after the parade. No evidence survives which would lead one to determine whether he did or did not attend, however.

After the parade, in the early evening hours the regiment boarded trains once again for the trip back to Camp Jackson. In the next several days records were checked, equipment was returned, pay vouchers reconciled, and a thousand other details finalized. During the wait, the men talked about what they had been through, the sights they had seen, the things they would remember, and others they could not forget. The last few days the veterans made promises to keep in touch and visit now and then, last handshakes, maybe a few hugs were exchanged, and a few tears were shed. On April 21, the last formation was called, and the men were dismissed.

It was now truly over. From the beginning in 1909, just ten years earlier, many of these men had been together through everything. They were now fast friends, even the ones from as far away as North Dakota and Illinois. Many were now missing from their number, never to return, but the kinship among the living would never be forgotten and the memories of their adventures together would be with them for the rest of their lives. The heart and soul of the outfits was Thomasville and Lexington and all the other towns of the original Third Brigade. The bonds that were forged among these men are the kind that can never be broken—or understood by outsiders.

One more thing was left to do—go home. On Monday, April 28, a gala reception was held in the hometown of each of the original companies. Wallace Stone, lately promoted to major, and several noncoms, hardly any of them Thomasville men, made speeches on this Easter Monday afternoon to enthusiastic crowds downtown. Food was served by the local residents, and a grand time was had by all. The same was true for Company A in Lexington. The soon-to-be famous Lexington-style barbecue was served to all the men and speeches made there too.

Of the ninety-two men in the Company L which went to Camp Sevier in 1917, there were about as many men at that Easter Monday celebration, but only forty-two from the original group. Many like Sam Myers and Marvin Lambeth were still convalescing, and others like Bob Little had been home for a while after being wounded. One or two of the boys from other towns decided to stay, but most of them returned to their homes in Kentucky, Virginia, Illinois, South Dakota, and Washington, DC.

[Benefitting from the locale of their home station, the Twenty-seventh Division paraded down Fifth Avenue in New York; this after parties and dinners were attended by famous actors and actresses, politicians, and businessmen. The parade was held on March 28, 1919, and was attended by as many as one million people who lined the streets many hours before the parade actually began.

Two scenes from the parade in downtown Charlotte welcoming the 120th home, April 16, 1919. From left above : Sen. Lee S. Overman, Mayor Frank McNinch, General Samson L. Faison, and Colonel Sidney Minor on the reviewing stand. Below: The regiment marches down Tryon Street past the reviewing stand. (Both Courtesy: The *Charlotte Observer*.)

The Twenty-seventh continued to be very active, even organizing a return to St. Quentin five years after the war ended. The division leaders even stated that they were the first to break the Hindenburg Line on that fateful day, but they are the only ones who make that claim. Historians all agree that it was the Thirtieth Division, with the 120th Infantry leading the way.]

AFTERWORD

Some years after the war, an American Legion was formed which was named for Hammett Harris and Dan Culbreth. Robert Little served several terms as commandant. The legion served the community up until the 1990s. In 1942, thirteen men met in front of Nance's Flower Shop on Salem Street and formed the William C. Miller Veterans of Foreign Wars Post 2756. Robert O. Little was elected the first commandant.

From 1919 until his death in 1947, Robert lived and worked in Thomasville. He loved to travel to the beach, go to baseball games, and was an active member of Unity Methodist Church where he was treasurer and Sunday school teacher. Like many others during the great depression, he was unemployed much of the time, but worked at one of the furniture factories when there was work to do.

The wound which took him out of the battles after September 29, 1918, continued to bother him for the rest of his life. In 1937 he kept a diary in which he wrote, "hope to get some compensation." Later that month, "Got letter from Charlotte, delay" and in February 1938, "Heard from Charlotte, no compensation."

In 1939, he landed a job at the post office as a letter carrier. During World War II, when an official envelope arrived for one of the people on his route, he would carry the letter to the door and stay while it was being read, making sure the recipient was not alone should there be bad news. He was well known around the town by almost everyone. He rarely, if ever, talked about his experiences in the military to anyone other than his comrades. On February 20, 1947, he complained of indigestion to his wife, son, and granddaughter. The next morning, he went to work as usual. While sitting on a stool waiting for his daily mail run to begin, he suffered a massive heart attack and died. He was fifty-eight.

~~~~

Sam Myers had his right leg blown off on September 29, 1918, as he was advancing toward Nauroy. His brother, Paul, seeing his brother down, pulled him out of the line of fire, stopped the bleeding, and went for help before returning to the fight. After his convalescence in England, Sam returned to Walter Reed Hospital in Washington, DC, where he received his discharge. In June 1922 he graduated from the Georgia School of Technology, Rehabilitation Division, in Atlanta, with a degree in accounting. After returning to Thomasville, he landed a job at the post office as a mailman despite the loss of the leg and continued at that job for over thirty years. He was an active member of Heidelberg United Church of Christ where, among other duties, he was a Sunday school teacher in a classroom, which was named in his honor. He died August 4, 1965, at the age of seventy-one.

~~~~

Marvin Lambeth did survive the war, but his convalescence took over five years, and he never recovered sufficiently enough to hold a job and support himself. He was in hospitals in France, Belgium, England, Baltimore, and finally at Walter Reed in Washington. Marvin did marry and started a family hoping to be able to return to work, but that never happened because he was unable to stand without crutches, and handicapped were not protected in those days. His meager disability allowance from the federal government was not enough. Fortunately, his nurse had become his wife, and she received another small pension to care for him. Still the family would not have survived, according to their son, if it had not been for the kindness of friends who brought food occasionally. Both of his sons entered the military during the Korean conflict; and Chauncy, the oldest, was killed in action there in 1951. Lambeth had a series of heart attacks beginning in 1948. Ten years later, at the veterans' hospital in Fayetteville, he suffered a final and fatal heart attack.

~~~~~

An interesting sidelight: Among Marvin's possessions was a photograph of the ship which finally brought him home in 1921, the USS *Olympia*. The photograph was taken at dockside from the stern of another ship in front of the *Olympia*. The picture shows a flag-draped casket being ceremoniously carried down the gangplank as the ship's company is assembled on deck. Another formation on the dock is waiting to receive the casket.

A search of the Internet revealed that the *Olympia* still exists and is a floating museum. The museum was interested in the photograph, and a copy was sent. The reply from the Independence Seaport Museum in Philadelphia stated,

> The photograph that you sent is not just of any soldier, sailor, marine, or airman from World War I being lifted off of the Olympia, it is actually the casket of the Unknown Soldier of World War I with his honor guard. The Olympia brought back the body of the Unknown Soldier from France in 1921 and delivered the remains to Arlington National Cemetery via the Washington Navy Yard. So, the image . . . was actually taken at Washington Navy Yard in November 1921. Due to the fact that this image depicts the first Unknown Soldier's arrival in America, it is quite extraordinary. Even more exciting is the angle that the photograph was taken from. In the Olympia collection, we have only a handful of photographs from this event, but all show the removal of the casket from the land. In the photograph that you sent in, the photographer must have been in a boat or ship next to the Olympia for this image to be taken from this location. It is such an evocative photograph that brings up many emotions.—Megan Good, director of the J. Welles Henderson Archives and Library

~~~~~

Mr. T. F. Harris, father of Hammet D. Harris visited his son's grave at Nine Elms Cemetery, Poperinghe, Belgium. Since Mr. Harris was a widower, the identity of the lady is uncertain but is probably his daughter Mamie, sister of Hammett.
Pvt. Harris was brought home and re-interred in Thomasville.

Beginning a year or so after the armistice, bodies of the fallen were returned to the United States if the next of kin so desired; for example, Pvt. Hammet D. Harris of Thomasville. In 1919, his father traveled to the Poperinge Cemetery near Ypres to visit his son's grave and arranged to have the body reinterred in his hometown. Many are still buried in Flanders Fields and elsewhere.

~~~~~

Major James A. Leonard returned to Lexington where he owned a hotel and café. In 1921 he ran for mayor of the city and defeated the incumbent. He was reelected twice more and during his tenure, his stature grew as improvements to the town were added. Gaining in popularity he ran for sheriff of the county in 1930 and defeated the incumbent, Fred Sink. Leonard was proud to have been elected to the office his father had also held. He was one of the most popular men in the county, and the future seemed bright for him.

On the evening of February 4, 1932, he and two friends had been drinking heavily and wrecked the automobile in which they were riding. Leonard seemed to blame a Good Samaritan named Neal Wimmer, nineteen, for the accident. Wimmer and his friend had stopped to help and gave the sheriff and his companions a ride back to town, but in his drunken state, the sheriff attempted to arrest Wimmer and ended up shooting him in the chest. One of Leonard's friends then tried to wrestle the gun from him, and the gun discharged twice, mortally wounding the sheriff. Wimmer was wounded but survived. Leonard's two friends, Younce and Brinkley, initially denied any knowledge of drinking but set the record straight next day in order to clear Wimmer of any blame.

Thus ended the career of one of the most popular and promising young men of Davidson County. From early adulthood, Leonard had been a popular leader and friend, politician and entrepreneur, soldier and public servant. The end of such a glorious career is tragic indeed. He was just three days shy of his forty-second birthday at the time of his death.

~~~~~

For Haymore Westmoreland's family, the sadness was not at an end. After the war was over, the grave, which had been carefully marked, could not be found. Haymore's father, Relius, had requested the return of his son to American soil. Two caskets were to be shipped by train to Thomasville, and one of them was to be Haymore, but when Relius arrived to claim the body, only one coffin had arrived and it was not his son's.

Twice more Mr. Westmoreland requested the return of his son's body, but they could not find it. Enlisting the aid of the Red Cross and other agencies, they finally found him—some of him, that is. After the war and after almost all of the Americans had gone home, a farmer had plowed up his remains and notified the British who were in control of that sector. What little they found—a dog tag, bits of a coat, a few bones, a right shoe, part of a gas mask, and little else—was reburied at the Poelcapelle British Cemetery in Belgium until final disposition could be made. No other body parts were found, not even the skull, but because of the dog tag and the fact that none other were found, it was definitely Haymore.

In 1924, after five long years of attempts to bring his son home, when confronted with this information and asked if he still wanted his son's remains returned, through trembling lips and tearful eyes, Haymore's father replied, "Leave him be." What remains of Haymore Westmoreland, the boy who only wanted to come home, had been turned over to the Americans and reinterred on October 23, 1923, in Flanders Field Cemetery, Waregem, Belgium, Plot A Row 3 Grave 17.

~~~~~

Bennett Cornelius suffered a fate similar to Westmoreland's. Both of the boys were killed within minutes of each other, and both bodies were taken to the rear for temporary burial. Unlike the case of Haymore Westmoreland, however, Cornelius's body was never found. His name is inscribed on the Tablet of the Missing at Flanders Field Cemetery, Waregem, Belgium. He is listed as "Missing in Action or Buried at Sea."

It seems that the original notification by the war department in Washington was used to describe the death of Cornelius, that being "missing in action." Subsequent official records later to be found at the National Archives apparently were not consulted as to the real cause of his death. A request to the American Battle Monuments Commission to change his inscription to "Killed in Action" was met with a form letter denying the request.

~~~~~

As the former Blues went home, their uniforms and souvenirs from their military days were stored and forgotten. Most of these men never discussed the great adventure in any detail even with their loved ones. After the war the headlines were all about the negotiations in Paris, Wilson's historic overtures (The Fourteen Points), the coming election, and Spanish influenza which was killing millions worldwide, even more than four years of war had done. The doughboys seemed content to let the past fade from consciousness.

Many relics were stored in trunks or bureaus to gather dust and be thrown out by the next generation. Helmets became door stops; children played with leggings, gas masks, and puttees thereby destroying them; pictures taken were never developed and chemically deteriorated on the roll of negatives, never to be seen; and the war itself faded from the public consciousness.

Unlike World War II, Vietnam, and especially the War between the States, there has never been a resurgence of interest in the Great War. It is as if the American public had given over any thought that this war held any importance for the country. The British and French, after all, played the major role in the Great War, so it seems that both they and the Americans regard it as their war and their victory. The Second World War, in which the United States played a bigger role, therefore holds the consciousness of the Americans, and the First World War is only an afterthought.

In addition, only a relatively few American authors have written histories of the monumental battles and sacrifices made by the men and women of the early twentieth century. Shelves in popular bookstores are crowded with narratives of the succeeding wars and its predecessors, but only a few books about World War I can be found on the same shelves, if any at all, and many of those by British authors.

Hometowns of the doughboys are also deficient in remembrances of the heroes of the Great War. For example, Burlington's American Legion is named for Sergeant Walter B. Ellis, Alamance County's (Company I, in the forefront of the attack on the Hindenburg Line) first KIA of the war, yet there are no remembrances of him, except one small picture which is difficult to find. Likewise, the local library has very little concerning the valor of their sons. A few newspaper articles and a couple of booklets are all that the public can access to honor those who gave so much for their fellow citizens.

Most Americans cannot relate any specific facts about the Great War other than who some of the belligerents were, and if pressed would state that the United States entered the war over the assassination of Archduke Frances Ferdinand or the sinking of the Lusitania, neither of which influenced President Wilson to ask for a declaration of war. Likewise, Americans have no knowledge of the events at home preceding the Great War—the troubles with Mexico in general and Pancho Villa in particular.

~~~~~

Those were exciting times, one in which the United States grew in stature and influence throughout the world. Americans were vigorous, ambitious, and imbued with that aspect which no foreigner can understand—*being* an American. These characteristics belonging to the American psyche brought us through the twentieth century, admittedly with a few setbacks, but at the end of the century a better country than when it began.

For Americans not to remember the valor and sacrifices made by the young men of the early 1900s is a disservice to their memory. They did not want this war, but when it came they were eager to fight it, to save democracy, to preserve the country's honor, to protect their family, or for whatever reason, they fought and died for the noblest of causes and did so unflinchingly. Those who returned to their homes would never be the same. They returned to a land for which they had given everything they had to give, and their progeny were the beneficiaries.

~~~~~

Twelve men of the Old Hickory Division in World War I were awarded the Congressional Medal of Honor, more than any other single division in the entire American Expeditionary Force.

> "The Division accomplished every task assigned to it. Not a single failure is recorded against it. Not a scandal occurred to mar the glory of its achievements. Duty to God, to country, and to home, well done, is the highest standard humanly attainable. The officers and men of the Thirtieth Division did their duty superbly. Their deeds and the example which they set are imperishable. North Carolina, South Carolina, and Tennessee may well be proud of their sons, both the living and the dead."—Major General E. M. Lewis, Commanding.

~~~~~

The Treaty of Versailles would not be signed until June 26, 1919. In fact it was never ratified by the American Senate. Americans considered the peace treaty too harsh for the losers, which proved to be the case. Thirteen of

Woodrow Wilson's Fourteen Points had not been accepted by the Allies, and the fourteenth was never implemented by our Congress, that being the League of Nations which we never joined. Almost three years after the armistice, Congress passed the Knox-Porter Resolution which formally brought an end to hostilities between the United States and Germany. It was signed into law by Wilson's successor, Warren Harding, on July 2, 1921.

The significance of the Great War cannot be understated. Almost every major world political event in the last one hundred years finds its roots there. For example, in Paris during the treaty negotiations was a young man from Indochina who asked for an audience with the American president and was rebuffed. He wanted some small concessions for his little country, but never got the chance to speak with anyone of any importance. His name was Ho Chi Minh and his country became Vietnam.

Other significant events which took place as a result of World War I are as follows:

- Every monarchy of Europe, except Great Britain, fell.
- The Bolshevik Revolution put the communists in power in Russia.
- The Ottoman Empire was broken up (but Turkey survived).
- Austria and Hungary were separated, Yugoslavia was formed from them.
- The Balkan states were rearranged.
- A corporal in the Great War, Adolf Hitler, embodied the outrage Germans felt toward the Treaty of Versailles, resulting in World War II.
- The United States, which had heretofore been an isolationist country, became a world power.
- The aid given to the British by the Japanese in China gave the latter a foothold in Southeast Asia and the Pacific. Japanese imperialism expanded over the next quarter century culminating in the sneak attack on Pearl Harbor in 1941.

TAPS

After the war, the boys of Company L were fast friends and formed honor guards at funerals of one of their number. One of the last gatherings of Company L may have been in 1947 at the funeral of First Lieutenant Robert O. Little. The obituary printed in the Thomasville Tribune for Tuesday, February 25, 1947, read as follows:

Full Military Honors Accorded Late Leader of Veterans' Groups
Impressive Rites held Sunday for Robert O. Little,
One of Few to Head Both Legion and VFW

Impressive church rites with full military honors marked funeral services held here Sunday afternoon at three o'clock for Robert O. Little, a veteran of World War I, a former commander of the American Legion and of Foreign Wars posts here, and since 1939 an employee of the United States Post Office here as a city mail carrier, whose death occurred Friday morning from a sudden heart attack suffered while he was at the post office.

Assembled at Unity Chapel Methodist church, of which he was a member, where the rites were held, was a capacity crowd, spreading out into the church yard. In charge of the services was his pastor, the Rev. A. James Clemmer, but in the church cemetery, where interment was made, final rites were in charge of members of the Legion and VFW, led by the respective commanders of the two posts, Howard Steed and Austin Elliott.

Music was by the combined choirs of Unity and Fair Grove Methodist churches, the members of which sang, "Rock of Ages" and "Ivory Palaces," while a quartet composed of Jesse Fritts, John Pope, Ed Hepler, and Howard Myers sang, "Abide with Me." Pianist was Miss Eloise Bodenheimer.

At attention was a color guard in charge of Floyd Hughes and James Sullivan were George Ellington, Robert Hundley, W. H. Jones, and Henry Early. Active pallbearers were: Mitt Veach, Arville Yarbrough, Sam and Paul Hall, John Brinkley*, Paul Green, C. H. Newby and Marvin M. Leonard, all members of Company L, the Thirtieth Division, World War I. Serving as honorary pallbearers was the entire group of Company L, together with other members of the Culbreth-Harris American Legion post and the William C. Miller post of the Veterans of Foreign Wars.

Robert O. Little wearing the uniform of the U. S. Post Office.
(Courtesy: Patsy Henderson)

In charge of the firing squad which fired a salute at the grave was Brice Barkley, who was assisted by Rudolph Blackwell, Eugene Branson, Julian Cranford, Dennis Howard, Harold Mabe, Odell Lambeth, Charles Wade, and Milton Jones. In the traffic detail were Harold Honeycutt, Ellis Hege, Dennis Westmoreland, Dugan Hundley, Paul Bryant, Harold Rachael, Jack Flowers, and from the City of Thomasville—Verlo Stamey, Willie Loftin, Clarence Walton, Ham Murphy, and Ben Johnson.

Taps were blown by Richard Johnson, Richard Foster, and Allen May.

Little was born on October 10, 1888, son of Robert O. *[sic. Actually Robert E.]* and Martha Jane Burrow Little and has been actively identified with the Culbreth-Harris post of the American Legion and the William C. Miller post of the Veterans of Foreign Wars. He was an active member of the Hilton Bible class of his church. He was also a member of the local lodge, Woodmen of the World.

Surviving are the widow, Mrs. Maud Turner Little; four sons: J. Carson Little of Lynchburg, Virginia; Robert C., Paul H., and Max E. Little—all of Thomasville. Two half sisters, Mrs. J. M. Presnell of Asheboro and Mrs. F. C. Burney of High Point, and one half brother, J. W. Wright of High Point, also survive as do fourteen grandchildren.

~~~~~

After Carlton Newby returned to the United States in August 1918 in order to train troops for overseas duty, he was promoted to major. His last command was at Camp Wadsworth, near Spartanburg, South Carolina, as commander of the 384th Infantry, Ninety-sixth Division, which only existed from September 1918 to January 1919. After leaving the army, he became a salesman for several furniture manufacturing concerns and died on March 22, 1951, while on a business trip to Tampa, Florida. His son, Carlton Jr., was with him when he died and accompanied the body home. Many of the men from Company L attended his funeral although many others had died before him.

~~~~~

Major Wallace Stone apparently left Thomasville for good just after the 1919 Easter Monday address to the crowds on the town square. He may have taken advantage of the opportunities for higher education provided by the federal government for veterans and became an attorney. A search of North Carolina obituaries revealed that he spent his last years at least in Swannanoa where he had close relatives. On March 14, 1967, he died at the veterans' hospital in Oteen from the effects of diabetes and was buried at the local Presbyterian Church Cemetery. The death certificate shows that he was also a veteran of WWII.

~~~~~

It is known that there was some personal animosity between Robert Little and Wallace Stone, but it's nature and exactly when it began are lost to history. Perhaps it had to do with the daylight patrol which cost the life of Little's best friend, Dan Culbreth, or Little's compassion for the wounded soldier back on September 29, or something else entirely. It is a fact that relations between the two men were cordial through the training at Camp Sevier and deteriorated thereafter.

Considering Little's popularity with the members of his former company as well as the citizenry, his absence from the newspaper account of the return to Thomasville on Easter Monday is puzzling. The same is true of the absence of any mention of Stone at the funeral of Little.

All other companies in the battalions recognized gassing as qualifying the wounded man to wear the wound chevron, but not a single gassing incident was thus listed by Captain Stone although many were thus wounded. All other official unit records do note the ones who were gassed but are curiously absent from Stone's. [In 2009, as this narrative was in its planning stages, a request to the National Personnel Records Center in St. Louis for recognition of the wound to Lieutenant Little was denied, there being no record of such an injury in Little's file. JL]

~~~~~

Clyde Tesh returned to Thomasville and married Hedda Harrison. His first job was with the Southern Railroad, but his dream was to go into business for himself. Eventually he landed a contract with in High Point producing all the printed advertising for the Southern Furniture Manufacturers Association. Brochures and pamphlets he produced were shipped across the nation and worldwide. Tesh, like his father before him, died young from heart attack in 1946 at age forty-eight. Company L was at the funeral.

~~~~~

As noted in Chapter 3, General Pershing was loyal to his own men in the regular army and not for National Guardsmen. Most of the glory, therefore, on the accounting of the war was heaped on the regular U.S. Army. The marines wrote their own history in blood at Belleau Wood. It is not surprising, therefore, that the battles by the First Army Division, the Twenty-Third, and a few others are the ones cited by most historians. But the battles fought by the Thirtieth Division were just as decisive, just as glorious as those fought by their comrades in arms, and ultimately helped in no small measure to bring on the end of the Great War.

~~~~~

Within a year of the armistice, plans were being made for a reunion of the Thirtieth Division. The location of the first reunion was never in question—Greenville, South Carolina—where the boys had trained for so long and had so many memories, good and bad. The event was not held on Armistice Day, but on the weekend of September 27-28, that being the closest weekend to their greatest battle.

The people of Greenville who had become fast friends with many of the men in 1917-1918 opened their doors and their hearts for this celebration of remembrance. Special editions of the newspaper highlighted each section of the division and their exploits. Unit histories were printed, and key officers were pictured.

At this reunion, Colonel Holmes B. Springs was elected president of the newly formed "Old Hickory Association." Springs was a South Carolinian originally from Georgetown but moved to Greenville in 1916 with the formation of the division. In its first official meeting the association endorsed the League of Nations and urged its adoption; chose Asheville, North Carolina, as the site of the second annual reunion; and called for good roads throughout the three states originally represented.

On the last weekend in September 1920, the reunion in Asheville was just as large as the one in Greenville. Side streets were designated for particular units while Patton Avenue hosted the big parade by the veterans on Saturday afternoon. Asheville's local newspapers ran extra editions welcoming the men and extolling their bravery, while remembering those who had fallen in battle.

The Old Hickory Association is still viable today, celebrating the soldiers of the division with reenactments and memorabilia. It's main focus is World War II, however, although a brief history is given. It can be accessed online.

~~~~~

During World War II the Thirtieth distinguished itself once again in Europe. It was judged the best overall division in the European Theater by General Dwight D. Eisenhower's staff historian, Colonel S. L. A. Marshall, who had been given the task of rating all the divisions in the European Theater. On March 16, 1946, Marshall wrote to General Hobbs, commander of the Thirtieth. "We placed 30th Division No. 1 on the list of first category divisions. It was the combined judgment of the approximately 35 historical officers . . . that the 30th had merited this distinction. It was our finding that the 30th had been outstanding in three operations and that we could consistently recommend it for citation on any one of these three occasions . . . we felt that the 30th was the outstanding infantry division of the ETO." [Their fathers would be proud of them.—JL]

~~~~~

The Old Hickory Division currently is headquartered in North Carolina as the Thirtieth Brigade due to the reorganization of the army away from the corps and division toward more flexible units. The 120th still exists also, but Company L is located elsewhere. The insignia for the 120th Regiment is a depiction of a cactus and the tunnel at Bellicourt on a blue background (for infantry), signifying the service on the border and France. The Latin phrase "VIRTUS INCENDIT VIRES" translates as "VIRTUE KINDLES STRENGTH."

~~~~~

The town of Thomasville continued to prosper throughout the twentieth century, even coming through the Great Depression fairly well. Thomasville Chair Company grew so rapidly and its product line expanded so much that the company was renamed Thomasville Furniture Industries, Inc.

Thomasville eventually became known as the "Chair City" reflecting its prominent place in the field. In 1922, a large chair was constructed of wood and leather and placed near the square downtown. After many years of deterioration it was replaced in 1951 by an even larger thirty foot concrete version. It still stands as the symbol of the city.

Even in recessions, the quality of furniture made in Thomasville, not only from Thomasville Furniture Industries but also from Erwin-Lambeth Furniture and others helped the companies to be a driving force in the industry, and is known worldwide. Numerous support industries such as carving, upholstery, mirrors, etc., were equally as prosperous as the big factories continued making quality American furniture.

Textiles were a huge part of the economy as well. Homer Regan, mentioned in the early part of this narrative, was one investor who helped open three hosiery mills at the same time in Thomasville just after the Great War. Regan Knitting was named for him, and there were many others as well.

All that changed as the century turned when, one by one, the factories began shutting down, their product lines being sent overseas. Today Thomasville's factories are mostly vacant. Plant C in the heart of town, once bustling, continues to make one line of furniture but the building itself is far from fully occupied. All of the support companies are gone and only one textile mill remains standing—vacant.

What the future holds for Thomasville and towns like it is anybody's guess. The men who formed Company L and the 120th infantry came back to the town and were able to land jobs to feed and clothe their families as did their children and grandchildren. Their dream was mostly fulfilled and our gratitude for their service is and always will be unbounded. One can only hope that their realization of that dream can once again be fulfilled.

APPENDIX

These are some of the Thomasville men from Company L who gave their lives for the American ideal. The photos of Hammet Harris and Harrison Sullivan were provided by Diane Murphy. The rest are courtesy of the *Charlotte Observer*. Other than Lieutenant Dan Culbreth, whose photo appears elsewhere in this narrative, no more pictures of the fallen have been found.

Hammet D. Harris
Killed in Action

Harrison Sullivan
Killed in Action

Pvt. Nickey Hopkins
Killed in Action

Pvt. Thomas G. Nance
Died of Disease

Pvt. John A. Myers
Died of Disease

A list of the fallen from Company L and their initial places of interment if known:

- Pfc. Hammet D. Harris; Thomasville, North Carolina; Aug. 4, 1918; killed at daylight by trench mortar; Nine Elms Cemetery, Poperinge, Belgium.
- 2nd Lt. Daniel C. Culbreth; Thomasville, North Carolina; Aug. 31, 1918, 1430; killed by rifle fire while advancing on enemy trench; Ypres sector, Lankhof Farm; Flanders, Belgium. Nine Elms Cemetery, Poperinge, Belgium.
- Pfc. Haymore Westmoreland; Thomasville, North Carolina; Aug. 31, 1918, 1430; killed by rifle fire while carrying message to platoon commander; Ypres sector, Lankhof Farm; Flanders, Belgium.
- Pfc. Reuben E. Davis; Thomasville, North Carolina; Aug. 31, 1918, 1430; killed by rifle fire while advancing on enemy; Ypres sector, Lankhof Farm, Flanders, Belgium.
- Pfc. Bennett Cornelius; Thomasville, North Carolina; Aug. 31, 1918, 1500; killed by rifle fire; Lankhof Farm, Flanders, Belgium.
- Pvt. Curtis Gurdner; Johnson City, Tennessee; Aug. 31, 1918, 1500; killed by rifle fire; Ypres sector, Lankhof Farm, Flanders, Belgium; Nine Elms Cemetery, Poperinge, Belgium.
- Pvt. Nealie W. Watts; hometown unknown; Sept. 2, 1918, 1500; killed by shell fire in front-line trench; Ypres sector, Lankhof Farm; Flanders, Belgium. Nine Elms Cemetery, Poperinge, Belgium.
- Pvt. William C. Lowery; Aug. 31, 1918, 1600; killed by rifle fire; Lankhof Farm, Flanders, Belgium. Nine Elms Cemetery, Poperinghe, Belgium.
- Pfc. John I. Smith; hometown unknown; Aug. 31, 1918, 1600; killed by rifle fire while advancing on enemy trenches; Lankhof Farm, Flanders, Belgium.
- Cpl. John R. Wilson; hometown unknown; Nine Elms Cemetery, Poperinge, Belgium.
- Pvt. Leslie C. Powell; hometown unknown; Aug. 31, 1918, 1700; killed by shell fire while on duty in front-line trenches; Ypres sector, Lankhof Farm, Flanders, Belgium.
- Pvt. William P. Smith; hometown unknown; Sept. 28, 1918, 0100; killed by shell fire; Bellicourt. He had only been with the company about ten days.
- Pvt. Hubert Upchurch; Buena Vista, Virginia; Sept. 28, 1918, 0100; killed by shell fire; Bellicourt.

- Pfc. Clarence I. Littlefield; Dalton, Kentucky; Sept. 29, 1918,0530; killed by shell fire while on tape awaiting orders to advance on enemy trenches in Hindenburg Line, Bellicourt, France Old Hickory Cemetery #3 near Bellicourt, France.
- Pfc. Dewey M. Sanders; hometown unknown; Sept. 29, 1918, 0545; killed by machine gun fire while waiting to advance on enemy lines; Hindenburg Line, Bellicourt, France.
- Pfc. Ernest Gurdner; Johnson City, Tennessee; Sept. 29, 1918, 0555; killed by shell fire while waiting to advance on enemy lines; Hindenburg Line, Bellicourt, France.
- Cpl. Lloyd C. Irvin; hometown unknown; Sept. 29, 1918, 0600; killed by shell fire while advancing on enemy trenches; Hindenburg Line, Bellicourt, France; Old Hickory Cemetery #3 near Bellicourt, France.
- Pvt. William H. Woods; Sept. 29, 1918, 0600; killed by shell fire while waiting to advance on enemy lines; Hindenburg Line, Bellicourt, France; Old Hickory Cemetery #3 near Bellicourt, France.
- Pvt. Jesse Slaven; Sept. 29, 1918, 0610; killed by shell fire while waiting to advance on enemy lines; Hindenburg Line, Bellicourt, France; Old Hickory Cemetery #3 near Bellicourt, France.
- Pvt. Lannie Lewis; hometown unknown; Nine Elms Cemetery, Poperinge, Belgium.
- Pvt. Leslie G. Fewell; hometown unknown; Nine Elms Cemetery, Poperinge, Belgium.
- Pfc. Jesse L. Barkley; Woodleaf, North Carolina; Sept. 29, 1918, 0625; killed by shell fire while advancing on enemy lines; Hindenburg Line, Bellicourt, France.
- Broadway, George L. Thomasville, North Carolina; Sept. 29, 1918; 0630; shell fire while advancing at Bellicourt; Old Hickory Cemetery #3 near Bellicourt, France.
- Sgt. Jessie B. Jones; Sept. 29, 1918, 0630; killed by machine gun fire while advancing on enemy trenches Hindenburg Line near Bellicourt; Old Hickory Cemetery #3 near Bellicourt, France.
- Pfc. Charlie Cook; Thomasville, North Carolina; Sept. 29, 1918, 0645; killed by shell fire while advancing on enemy trenches, Hindenburg Line, Bellicourt, France; Old Hickory Cemetery #3 near Bellicourt, France.
- Pfc. Harvey J. Ramsey; North Carolina; Sept. 29, 1918, 0645; killed by shell fire while advancing on enemy trenches; Hindenburg Line; Bellicourt, France.

- Pfc. Mickey W. Hopkins; Thomasville, North Carolina; Sept. 29, 1918, 0645; killed by shell fire while advancing on enemy trenches; Hindenburg Line; Bellicourt, France; Old Hickory Cemetery #3 near Bellicourt, France.
- Cpl. James H. Sloan; Sept. 29, 1918, 0700; killed by shell fire while advancing on enemy trenches; Hindenburg Line, Bellicourt, France.
- Pvt. William M. Littrell; Indiana; Sept. 29, 1918, 0700; killed by shell fire while advancing on enemy trenches; Hindenburg Line, Bellicourt, France.
- Pfc. Eugene Pate; Evansville, Indiana; Sept. 29, 1918, 0700; killed by shell fire while advancing on enemy trenches; Hindenburg Line, Bellicourt, France; Old Hickory Cemetery #3 near Bellicourt, France.
- Pvt. Doctor T. Norman; hometown unknown; ; Old Hickory Cemetery #3 near Bellicourt, France
- Pvt. Ben C. Ellis; Thomasville, North Carolina; Sept. 29, 1918, 1100; killed by shell fire while advancing on the enemy; Bellicourt; Old Hickory Cemetery #3 near Bellicourt, France.
- Pvt. John W. Moore; Autryville, South Carolina; Oct. 1, 1918; no witness to death; Bellicourt.
- Pvt. James Reneau; Jefferson City, Tennessee; about October 7.
- 1st Lt. Gordon C. Gillespie; Memphis, Tennessee; Oct. 18, 1918, 0500; killed by shell fire while going from company HQ to battalion HQ; St. Martin Reverie, France. Nine Elms Cemetery, Poperinge, Belgium.
- Pvt. Willie W. Wicker; hometown unknown; Cemetery Unknown.
- Pvt. John Crow; died of wounds in hospital.
- Pvt. Elmer Harper; died of wounds in hospital.
- Pvt. Robert Hensley; North Carolina; died of wounds in hospital, Sept. 2, 1918; Gunshot wound right hip.
- Pvt. John C. Martin; died of disease in hospital.
- Pvt. Herbert Neal; died of disease in hospital.
- Noah Pope, Unknown
- Lt. Clare McCaskey, Chicago, Illinois; Assigned Co. K after the death of Ben Dixon and was killed in action 10/10/1918. After the return of the 120th to the United States, the Charlotte Observer published a letter from his mother who was desperately trying to find out how her son had died. She was unaware that her son had been transferred to the Asheboro Company.

The American Battle Monument to the 27th and 30th Divisions at Bellicourt, France.

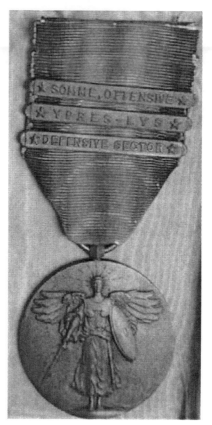

The Victory Medal of the Great War authorized by the Department of the Army
in 1920 and issued to all regular army and national army service men in 1921.
The top is a multicolored ribbon to which clasps are attached. Only eleven clasps
were authorized, the Hindenburg Line being included in the Somme Offensive
above. The reverse side lists the Allies and the words "THE GREAT WAR FOR
CIVILIZATION." This medal belonged to Clyde Tesh. (Courtesy Jay Harry Tesh)

In October 1918 W. O. Burgin, chairman of the Davidson County Council of Defense, proposed a monument to remember the war dead. The World War I monument for the Davidson men killed in the Great War is located on the square in Lexington, North Carolina. (Photo by the author)

SOURCES

All references to the Militia Act of 1903 were obtained from online sources such as www.history.army.mil/documents.

The Dispatch, Lexington, North Carolina; 1909-19; Microfilm-Davidson County Library, Lexington, NC.

Mary Green Matthews and M. Jewel Sink; *Wheels of Faith and Courage*, North Carolina; Hall Publishing Co., High Point, NC; 1951.

North Carolina Department of Archives, Raleigh, North Carolina. Lt. Col. Sion Harrington.

World War I records, North Carolina Department of Archives, Colonel Joseph Hyde Pratt collection.

World War I records, North Carolina Department of Archives, Major General J. Van B. Metts collection.

R. Jackson Marshall; *Memories of World War I; North Carolina Doughboys on the Western Front*; Division of Archives and History, North Carolina Department of Cultural Resources; 1998,

The Davidsonian, 1911-1915. Published first in Thomasville then Lexington. Microfilm—Davidson County Library, Thomasville, NC.

National Archives and Records Administration, (NARA II); College Park, Maryland.; 30th Division Collection.

The Thomasville Tribune on microfilm. Davidson County Library, Thomasville, NC.

The Thomasville News Times on microfilm. Davidson County Library, Thomasville, NC

"North Carolina in the World War"; An Address by Walter Clark Jr., Captain in 30th U.S. Division, delivered before the North Carolina Bar Association at Blowing Rock, NC, July 5, 1924. Published by the Charlotte Chamber of Commerce, 1924.

Barbara Tuchman; *The Guns of August*; Ballantine Books, New York; 1962.

Barbara Tuchman; *The Zimmerman Telegram*; Ballantine Books, New York; 1958.

Elmer A. Murphy and Robert S. Thomas; *The Thirtieth Division in the World War*; (1936)

The Papers of Colonel Joseph Hyde Pratt located in the North Carolina Archives.